PELICAN BOOKS

The Economist Economics

Rupert Pennant-Rea is editor of *The Economist*. He has degrees in economics from Trinity College, Dublin, and the University of Manchester. He has worked for an employers' organization in Ireland and a trade union in Britain. From 1973 to 1977 he worked at the Bank of England, before joining *The Economist* as its economics correspondent. He became the paper's economics editor in 1981, and was appointed editor in February 1986. He has been a regular consultant to the World Bank and principal editor of its *World Development Report*.

Clive Crook is economics editor of *The Economist*. He was educated at Magdalen College, Oxford, and the London School of Economics. He was an official in the monetary policy division of the Treasury, and private secretary to the government's Chief Economic Adviser, before joining the editorial staff of *The Economist* in 1983. After a spell in London as economics correspondent he moved to the paper's Washington office. He was made economics editor in February 1986.

Rupert Pennant-Rea
and Clive Crook

The Economist Economics

Penguin Books

Penguin Books Ltd, Harmondsworth, Middlesex, England
Viking Penguin Inc., 40 West 23rd Street, New York, New York 10010, U.S.A.
Penguin Books Australia Ltd, Ringwood, Victoria, Australia
Penguin Books Canada Limited, 2801 John Street, Markham, Ontario, Canada L3R 1B4
Penguin Books (N.Z.) Ltd, 182–190 Wairau Road, Auckland 10, New Zealand

First published by The Economist Newspaper Limited 1985
Revised edition published in Pelican Books 1986

Made and printed in Great Britain by
Richard Clay (The Chaucer Press) Ltd, Bungay, Suffolk
Filmset in Monophoto Times

Contents

Preface

Economics is not a settled science with many undisputed truths; some people would argue that it is not a science at all. It reacts to changes in the real world, its theorists refine their theories. New schools of thought emerge to challenge conventional wisdom. Computers and mathematics allow today's economists to do things that their predecessors never dreamt of.

This book describes where economics has got to during the 1980s, and where it seems to be going. It is based on a series of briefs first published in *The Economist* in 1984. Much of the material has been reworked to turn the briefs into a coherent book. We hope it will refresh memories and help newcomers.

Many people have had a hand in producing the book. Our thanks to several colleagues on *The Economist*, who helped with charts and statistical material. We received much useful advice from David Begg of Worcester College, Oxford, who acted as academic mentor.

1 Introduction: Changing times

'Economics,' said the American economist Jacob Viner, 'is what economists do.' His definition is usefully vague, because the subject never stands still. Contrary to popular opinion, economics is not just an ivory-tower preserve. Much of its inspiration comes from changes in the real world, and always has done.

In the eighteenth century, Adam Smith wrote *The Wealth of Nations* in the early years of Britain's industrial revolution, arguing that countries and people would grow richer if only they allowed free markets to work. In the nineteenth century, David Ricardo tried to explain the poverty of the masses. Karl Marx carried the argument through to a vision of 'inevitable' revolution. John Maynard Keynes responded to the mass unemployment of the 1930s, saying that the macroeconomic management of demand was needed to sustain growth and jobs. All of them were influenced by the events of their time: different events, producing different intellectual ideas.

In public at least, economic controversy dies down when economies are doing well. It did so in the 1950s and 1960s, with the apparent success of the Keynesian formula. Most politicians and many economists no doubt oversimplified that formula, but its essence was beguiling. Governments believed they could achieve their goals by the precise use of just a few policies. In particular, they thought that fiscal policy – public spending and taxation – had a direct and predictable effect on output. If growth was flagging and unemployment rising, government should increase its spending and/or reduce taxes.

This approach carried a risk that Keynes himself had well understood: the risk of inflation. To this, Keynesian economists had a ready response. If the economy overheated and inflation started to rise, the government should tighten its fiscal policy and raise interest rates a bit, and inflation would then subside. If need be, some economists also advocated more direct methods of restraining inflation – wage and price controls administered by the government.

As for that other concern, the external balance of payments, there too economists seemed to provide an answer. Any persistent deficit on the current account was a sign that the exchange rate was overvalued. Faster productivity growth and slower cost inflation at home, if achieved, would justify the exchange rate and restore external balance. Failing that, the government could eventually devalue the currency.

This philosophy was not shared by every economist. Some continued to believe the old religion of classical economics. They stressed the role of monetary policy in determining total spending, and they advocated microeconomic measures to improve the economy's efficiency at the level of its individual markets. In particular they emphasized the need for a flexible labour market; wage adjustments could then be relied upon to hold the economy at full employment. These notions were not altogether ignored by the prevailing orthodoxy. But its emphasis remained heavily macroeconomic, with a bias towards fiscal policy. For as long as it got results, it was hard to challenge.

For roughly twenty years, the results were undeniable. Economies that had suffered mass unemployment in the 1930s found themselves with jobless rates of about 2 per cent, sometimes less. Real incomes grew steadily: 'mass prosperity' moved from being a dream to a cliché. Governments seemed to be munificent, their economic advisers wise.

The fact that government spending was growing rapidly seemed, in the 1960s, to be of little significance. As figure 1.1 shows, public expenditure rose as a proportion of G.N.P. in all the main groups of countries belonging to the Organization for Economic Co-operation and Development (O.E.C.D.). The emphasis that governments in the 1980s place on cutting public

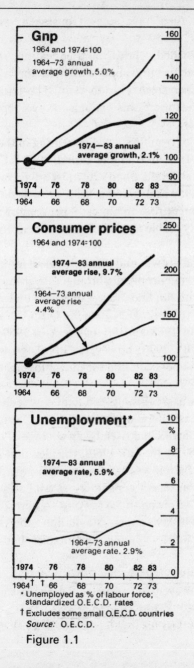

Figure 1.1

spending would then have seemed mistaken, even ridiculous. Taxpayers were ready to pay more for many things that governments provided – health and education, roads, pensions and armies. Even after these bills were paid, the average taxpayer was growing richer from year to year. The pace of economic growth meant that there was enough for everybody to increase their real incomes.

The first signs of trouble started appearing in the late 1960s. In the twenty-four rich and largely capitalist O.E.C.D. countries, real gross national product had grown by an average 5.5 per cent a year between 1959 and 1966; in 1967, growth slowed to 3.8 per cent. Unemployment rose to almost 3 per cent of the workforce, having been fairly stable at around 2.5 per cent for the previous five years.

These figures on growth and unemployment look enviable now; at the time they were deeply disturbing. Governments responded on standard Keynesian lines, increasing their budget deficits. The response seemed to work: G.N.P. in the O.E.C.D. countries grew by 5.4 per cent in 1968 and 5.1 per cent in 1969, while jobless rates fell back. By 1970, however, G.N.P. growth had again slowed, to only 3.1 per cent, and the unemployment rate exceeded 3 per cent.

While growth was weakening, economies were showing another symptom of ill health. Inflation was rising. Consumer prices in the O.E.C.D. countries had risen by an average of only 2 per cent a year in 1953–65. By the late 1960s, the idea that slower growth brought lower inflation was starting to disappear. In 1970, when G.N.P. growth slackened, consumer-price inflation in O.E.C.D. countries carried on rising to 5.6 per cent. A new word was added to the dictionary of economics: 'stagflation', the combination of stagnation and inflation that many economists had come to think was impossible.

The stagflationary year of 1970 worried all O.E.C.D. governments. However, they were concerned less about inflation than unemployment. They reflated demand again, and O.E.C.D. G.N.P. growth picked up to 3.6 per cent in 1971, 5.4 per cent in

1972 and 6.1 per cent in 1973. Although that sounds impressive, the consequences were not. Unemployment was slower to respond; in 1973 it was still higher than it had been in 1970. But inflation was quick to rise, even though more governments were trying to contain it with wage and price controls. In the second half of 1973 – before oil prices shot up – consumer prices in O.E.C.D. countries rose at an annual rate of 10.3 per cent.

The end of consensus

The inflationary surge and stubborn unemployment brought the Keynesian consensus to an end. That happened to coincide with two other developments in the real world that were changing the way that economists and governments thought.

The quadrupling of oil prices in the northern winter of 1973–74

The rise was orchestrated by the O.P.E.C. cartel, but market forces were moving that way anyway. Demand for oil had been growing faster than new discoveries for roughly five years, so prices were bound to rise. Economic growth fuelled by cheap energy was no longer possible. And in the short term, the quadrupling of oil prices meant that roughly 2 per cent of gross world product was suddenly transferred from the pockets of consumers in the O.E.C.D. countries to a handful of oil producers who could not spend it so quickly. Real demand was cut even as inflation spurted – stagflation with a vengeance.

The floating of exchange rates

Inflation at anything faster than 2–3 per cent was likely to strain the system of fixed exchange rates agreed at the Bretton Woods conference of 1944. Countries were not all inflating at the same pace, so their costs got out of line – and they did so more quickly when inflation speeded up. In 1967, consumer-price inflation in the seven biggest O.E.C.D. economies ranged from West

Germany's 1.4 per cent to Japan's 4.0 per cent. By 1971 that gap of 2.6 percentage points between the slowest and fastest inflaters had widened to 6.6 points, between Canada's 2.8 per cent and Britain's 9.4 per cent. (Strictly, the prices that matter for exchange rates are those of traded goods: they, too, were rising at increasingly different speeds.)

Governments made one last attempt to keep their currencies fixed. At the Smithsonian meeting in Washington in December 1971, they agreed on a new set of exchange rates. The dollar was devalued by 10 per cent; the D-mark and the yen were both revalued. These changes were widely agreed to be necessary to correct trade imbalances. However, the foreign exchange markets now knew that 'fixed' rates could be changed, provided enough money was pushed against them. The Smithsonian parities were soon challenged. Within two years, the major currencies were all floating.

The switch from fixed to floating exchange rates coincided with a relaxation of controls on international capital movements. The world was suddenly having to cope with the huge financial surpluses of O.P.E.C. oil exporters. These had to be 'recycled' back to borrowers in the O.E.C.D. countries and the developing world. The job was left largely to commercial banks and private markets.

With so much money sloshing about, exchange rates were bound to become more volatile. Money managers realized that they could win and lose millions through hourly movements in exchange rates that had previously not changed for years on end. They became far more sensitive to macroeconomic policies that might cause exchange rates to move. And they were particularly sensitive to inflation, which rose to an O.E.C.D. average of 13.4 per cent in 1974, with a spread among the seven biggest economies that ranged from West Germany's 7.0 per cent to Japan's 24.5 per cent.

Governments also found themselves in a different world. Faster inflation and slower growth made it harder for them to judge the stance of their policies. Were interest rates rising because inflation was rising, or because monetary policy was tightening? Did a larger budget deficit boost the volume of demand, or did it simply show the differential effects of rising prices on government revenue and spending? The old certainties, brought about by low inflation and financial stability, no longer applied. The times demanded fresh thinking.

New conundrums

The early 1970s marked a break with the post-war past, and O.E.C.D. economies have done much worse since then. As figure 1.1 shows, growth has been slower, inflation faster and unemployment higher. Some economists therefore see the pre-1973 period as a golden age that could be regained if governments reverted to the same Keynesian policies. They believe that governments have generally restrained their fiscal policies too much, and that the widespread adoption of monetary targets since the mid-1970s has been a mistake. Those who take this view tend to see the American boom in 1983–4 as a direct consequence of President Reagan's large budget deficits and the relaxation of monetary restraint in mid-1982.

Other economists disagree. They argue that post-1973 difficulties were the outcome of pre-1973 policies: only when the damage done by those policies has been repaired will economies again blossom. Economists of this persuasion think that governments now play such a big role in economic life that high taxes, controls and regulation have sapped the ability of the private sector to deliver rapid growth. They also believe that the rapid inflation of the 1970s has done harm that it will take many years to eradicate.

This disagreement is usually presented in Keynesian-versus-monetarist terms, with each camp blaming the other for the economic failings of the past dozen years. In fact, neither camp is as monolithic as it is made to sound. Nor are they concerned just to re-fight old battles. Enough has changed in the real world for Keynesians and monetarists to find some common ground, and for new ideas to emerge that cannot be easily pigeonholed.

Take exchange rates as an example. Until 1973 the world had never known flexible exchange rates coupled with such a volume of internationally mobile money. The switch raised economic questions that had never been asked, and opened up new fields for research. The factors determining exchange rates are still only partly understood. So are the ramifications for trade, interest rates, prices, profits, etc.

Keynesians in particular have had to adapt their views to the new world of floating rates. Keynes's major work, *The General Theory of Employment, Interest and Money*, was couched in terms of a closed economy without international trade. The neo-Keynesian view on capital flows and exchange rates has borrowed from non-Keynesian monetary (though not necessarily monetarist) economists. The use of all these terms to describe various schools of thought shows that the Keynesian–monetarist distinction is usually too simple.

Unemployment is another area where economists have a lot of new delving to do. In virtually every O.E.C.D. country, jobless rates are much higher than they were in the early 1970s. Slower economic growth is part of the explanation, no doubt. But researchers are also looking at the influence on jobs of real wages, state benefits and taxes, information about vacancies, etc. They are treating the labour market as the sum of numerous individual bargains, and then looking at the microeconomic factors which affect such bargaining.

Few if any of the new developments in economics are truly path-breaking. They employ concepts that have been around for years; to that extent they can be understood by people whose economics has grown rusty. But the methods of economics – its language and its analytical tools – have changed in ways that can be perplexing to outsiders. For better or worse these changes have altered the very nature of the subject.

The way it is done

Truth in economics is never easy to establish, but the search for it takes three main forms:

Theory through words

Until the mid-1960s, the main way for economists to communicate with each other was through the written word. The words were supplemented by diagrams, ranging from simple supply and demand curves through to more complicated ones, like those dealing with international trade. Statistics were presented in tables or in time-series charts that tried to show links between, for example, money and prices.

The object of the exercise was to develop theories about how the world worked. That involved some attempt to quantify the effects of, say, a change in spending on growth and employment. But most economists were sceptical that they could quantify accurately. Writing in 1960, Professor Harry Johnson thought it 'inevitable that economic policymakers and commentators must rely to a large extent on guessing at the magnitude of economic effects'. Yet eleven years later he claimed that the ability to quantify and predict 'now constitutes the economists' main claim to superiority as a profession over the general run of intelligent men with an interest in economic problems'. Johnson's growing confidence was due to the rise of the other two methodologies.

Theory through mathematics

During the twentieth century, the verbal tradition in economics has gradually been superseded by the use of mathematics (and particularly calculus). Often this is just for convenience: to write

$$C_t = a + bY_{t-1}$$

is quicker than writing that consumption in a particular period is determined by some constant number plus some fraction of what income was in the previous period. Every subject, from cooking to nuclear physics, has its own shorthand. Non-economists must surely welcome anything that makes economics less windy.

However, mathematics is increasingly used for more compli-cated reasons. The winner of the 1983 Nobel prize for economics, Professor Gerard Debreu, made his name by establishing the theoretical circumstances in which a set of competitive markets could achieve simultaneous equilibrium. This was a major intellectual feat, impossible without mathematics; but it was also extraordinarily arcane, appealing only to the purist and not at all to the practitioner. Many sceptics wonder whether the Debreu approach makes economics any more relevant or fruitful a sub-ject.

Testing through econometrics

This is the newest methodology, made possible by the de-velopment of computers. The computer can apply mathematical formulas to piles of statistics, to assess the relationship (if any) between variables that economic theorists believe to be linked. In principle this is obviously useful. But sceptics fear what they call 'data-mining' – using econometrics indiscriminately to establish relationships which are then given a spurious significance. It may be possible to show an excellent econometric link between the output of beer cans in one year and gross domestic product in the following year. But that is no guide to anything, unless theorists can first explain how beer cans affect G.D.P.

Mathematics and econometrics now dominate the academic literature of economics and the teaching of the subject in univer-sities. These changes have made economics less accessible, al-though most of the results of new work can still be expressed in words and simple diagrams. However, this does mean that policymakers often have to take the advice of economists on trust, because they cannot understand how their advisers reached their conclusions. In such circumstances, politicians may be tempted to ignore the advice if it happens to conflict with their own preference.

The move towards mathematics and econometrics has failed to impress some distinguished economists. Professor Wassily

Leontief, Nobel laureate in 1973, has analysed the articles in the *American Economic Review* between 1972 and 1981. Table 1.1 shows the trend – and Professor Leontief did not like it. 'Page after page of professional economic journals,' he complained in a letter to the American magazine, *Science*, 'is filled with mathematical formulas leading the reader from sets of more or less plausible but entirely arbitrary assumptions to precisely stated but irrelevant conclusions.'

Younger economists – particularly academics – hear these criticisms but reject them. Most believe that their subject is developing in fruitful ways. They do not see the new methodologies as a threat to the 'real economics' of theory and observation – only to the amateur economists who have failed to keep up.

Table 1.1

Contents of articles published in the American Economic Review	1972–6 (%)	1977–81 (%)
Mathematical models without any data	50.1	54.0
Analysis without any mathematical formulation and data	21.2	11.6
Statistical methodology	0.6	0.5
Empirical analysis based on data researched by author	0.8	1.4
Empirical analysis using indirect statistical inference based on data published or researched elsewhere	21.4	22.7
Empirical analysis not using indirect statistical inference, based on data researched by author	0.0	0.5
Empirical analysis not using indirect statistical inference, based on data published or researched elsewhere	5.4	7.4
Empirical analysis based on artificial simulations and experiments	0.5	1.9

Source: Science

2 Defining demand

Old Cambridge lags, who learned economics in 1935–65, will be distressed to hear that modern theorists do not believe that effective demand was efficiently analysed by Keynes. But you may begin to understand more modern theories about it if you start with Keynes's Oxford near-contemporary, Sir John Hicks.

Theorists are simplifiers. Their job is to discard complexities and details that get in the way of understanding what really matters. If they discard the wrong things, their theories will not stand up to testing, nor to the logic of other theorists. By convention, the elementary theory of aggregate demand initially ignores international trade and assumes (most of the time) that prices are stable. Those issues are the flesh that will be added in later chapters to the bare bones of demand theory.

There are four bones to keep in mind. Two are in the goods market – consumption and investment; added together, they are equal to total demand. Two are in the money market, because demand manifests itself through money. The demand for money comes in two forms: transactions and speculative, fancy terms which will be explained shortly. Government spending, another big component of demand, will be brought into chapter 6; for now, it is assumed to be constant.

Using these four notions, economists can throw light on familiar real-world questions: what effect do lower interest rates have on demand? What happens if governments cut taxes on income? By itself, theory provides no conclusive answers; but at least it allows them to be discussed in a common language.

Start with the goods market, and what determines consumption and investment.

Consumption is obviously affected by income; as chapter 6 will show, it is also affected by, for example, interest rates. But the simplest consumption function has only one variable: as income increases, so does consumption.

Economists have little difficulty defining and measuring consumption, but the meaning of 'income' is less clear. In any particular period, people do not spend according to their income in that period: a self-employed person on holiday is earning nothing, but may be spending more than at any other time of the year. Theorists have agreed that income is a long-run notion, perhaps extending over a person's lifetime. Professor Milton Friedman coined the term 'permanent income'; people will not change spending patterns unless they think their income has changed in some lasting way.

Investment is a trickier concept. Advanced theories show it is determined by several different factors. In this chapter, interest rates are deemed the critical influence. If they rise, firms will be reluctant to hold as many stocks (inventories) as before, and may also decide to shelve some capital projects which no longer seem to justify the cost of financing them. Companies are always looking at the 'opportunity cost' of what they are doing: the alternative to investing in new plant or extra stocks may be to put money into a bank, which becomes more attractive when interest rates rise.

Cash in hand

So far total demand could hardly be simpler: it has two components, consumption and investment, affected by two variables, income and interest rates. Now bring money into it.

An old joke has three men marooned on a desert island, with a tin of beans but no way of opening it. 'Make a fire and boil it till it bursts,' suggests the physicist. 'Find a stone and bash it,' offers the engineer. The economist ponders a while and then provides his solution: 'Assume a tin opener.'

The assumptions made in the monetary part of simple demand theory are a bit like that. First, that the money supply is fixed by the government; second, that prices are stable. Given the obvious difficulties that governments have in restraining the money supply and avoiding inflation, these assumptions must be removed in due course. For the moment, they provide a consistency between the goods market – where consumption and investment are both treated as real values – and the money market.

The demand for money is therefore a demand for real money and it takes two forms:

Transactions demand

This is shorthand for how much money people need to have available for spending. They receive income infrequently – say, in a monthly pay cheque – but spend it pretty continuously. For convenience they need cash and a bank account – the two main components in most measures of the money supply. This type of demand for money is obviously affected by the absolute level of income: the richer a country, the more it spends.

Speculative demand

As well as needing money for spending, people choose between holding money and buying financial assets. Economists avoid the colloquial term 'investing', which to them means adding to the stock of physical capital rather than shuffling bank deposits, shares, life assurance policies, etc.

The speculative demand for money arises because people shift between money and bonds, the simplified choice that theory gives them. They shift according to changes in interest rates. Higher interest rates mean a higher return on holding bonds, and a bigger opportunity cost against holding cash or interest-free bank deposits. So when interest rates rise, the speculative demand for money falls.

Now the simple model of aggregate demand is starting to take shape. Its two financial variables, the transactions and speculative demand for money, are influenced by income and interest rates respectively. Those are the same two factors that affect consumption and investment. The whole model can therefore be built on the common ground of income and interest rates.

Joining up

Look first at the effects of the market in money on the market in goods. If the supply of money is increased, interest rates will initially fall. Lower rates boost investment, so income rises. But that does not yet mean a new equilibrium, because higher income increases the transactions demand for money – which will then pull up interest rates a bit, trimming investment back. So the final boost to income will be smaller than the initial boost.

Now look at the effects of a change in the goods market on the money market. If consumer spending increases – as a result, say, of tax cuts – total demand will initially rise. But that will increase the demand for money, so raising interest rates. Higher rates will trim investment and consumer spending; once again, when a new equilibrium is eventually reached the final increase in demand is less than the initial one. How much less is a matter of fierce debate, of course, because it is the heart of fiscal-versus-monetary disagreement.

That whole issue becomes clearer if the model of aggregate demand is taken a stage further. It is useful to see how the market in money affects the market in goods, and vice versa; it is much more useful to combine them, so that both markets can simultaneously reach their equilibrium. This is a bit more complicated, but well worth doing.

The year after John Maynard Keynes published his *General Theory*, another British economist, Professor (later Sir) John Hicks, distilled what he saw as the essence of Keynes's ideas into a diagram. For more than thirty years it helped to dominate the teaching of macroeconomics; although it has fallen from favour recently, many of the new developments in economic thought can be explained in its terms.

Hicks charts

The Hicks diagram develops out of two others dealing with the market for goods and then for money. Figure 2.1 takes the goods market. Starting in the bottom-left quadrant, it shows a straightforward identity, savings (s) = investment (I), which occurs at any point on the 45° line. The top-left quadrant shows I as a function of interest rates (R).

The bottom-right quadrant gives the consumption function, though it does so indirectly via savings. As income (Y) rises, so do savings, but by less than the increase in Y: this leaves room for consumption to rise as Y does.

These three quadrants can now be used to help fill the fourth. The top-right quadrant is the one that really matters, because it

Figure 2.1

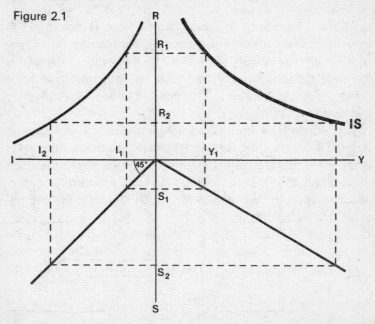

contains the two common variables, income and interest rates.

Start at some point on the investment axis, say I_1. The investment function shows that this is consistent with a particular rate of interest, R_1. Now run down to the 45° line, then across to S_1, then into the bottom-right quadrant (the consumption function), then up to Y_1, and so into the top-right quadrant. When that line reaches the interest rate R_1, it has established a point at which the goods market is in equilibrium at some particular combination of interest and income.

The same procedure can be repeated from another point on the investment function, where higher investment I_2 is compatible with a lower interest rate R_2. This will establish a new point in the top-right quadrant.

Join the two points up and there is the is line: it defines the goods market equilibrium at different combinations of interest rates and income.

Figure 2.2 deals with the money market. This time start in the top-left quadrant. It shows that the speculative demand for real

Figure 2.2

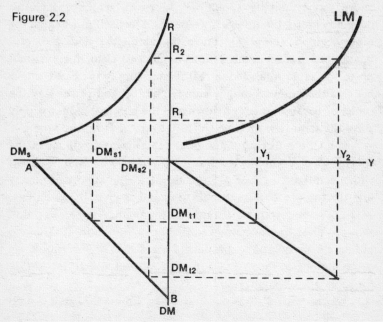

money falls as the interest rate rises. The line curves in towards the origin because (a) at very low interest rates, people become indifferent to holding money or bonds, so the demand-curve flattens out; and (b) at very high interest rates, people will try to cut their speculative holdings of money to a minimum, so the demand curve becomes nearly vertical. The transactions demand for money, in the bottom-right quadrant, is deemed simply a constant share of income – so it rises as income rises.

The bottom-left quadrant brings the two components together, but in a different way from the corresponding part of the IS figure. In the goods market, equilibrium requires that planned savings equal planned investment – represented by a 45° line drawn from the origin. But in the money market, equilibrium requires that the speculative and transaction demands for real money add up to the total real money supply. That is shown by a 45° line drawn from axis to axis.

This line shows, for example, that if the transactions demand for money is zero, the speculative demand must account for the entire money supply (point A). Likewise, if the speculative demand is zero, the transactions demand by itself must equal the money supply (point B). Travelling along the line, geometry guarantees that all combinations of the two elements must add up to the same total. If the real money supply increases, either because the nominal money supply goes up and prices stay the same, or because prices go down and the nominal money supply stays the same, the 45° line shifts out farther from the origin.

Again, these three quadrants are the means to filling in the fourth, which combines interest rates and income. Start at DM_{s1}, with an interest rate of R_1; run down to the supply-of-money line, then across to DM_{t1}, then up to Y_1 and on up to the level of R_1.

Do the same from a different starting point, DM_{s2} and R_2, and that produces a second point in the top-right quadrant. The two points can be joined to produce the LM line, which shows the combinations of income and interest rates at which the market for money is in equilibrium.

Now the model's various parts can be manipulated simultaneously. Looking at figure 2.3, suppose the LM curve shifts to the right because the real money supply has increased. Why does this shift the LM curve? Because interest rates fall when the real money supply increases, as the way of persuading people to hold more money at any given level of income. The same point can be understood from the opposite direction: for any particular interest rate, people will need higher real incomes if they are to increase their holdings of money.

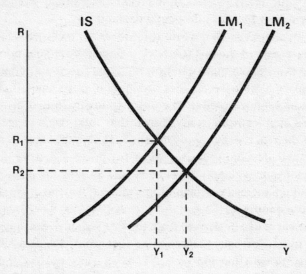

Figure 2.3

For a fuller demonstration of how the LM curve will shift, use figure 2.2 to work out what happens when the 45° line in the bottom-left quadrant shifts out to the left, signifying an increase in the real money supply. When the LM curve shifts to the right, from LM_1 to LM_2, figure 2.3 shows that interest rates will fall from R_1 to R_2 and total income will rise from Y_1 to Y_2.

The same procedure can be followed for a shift in the IS curve. A shift to the right means that, at any given interest rate, demand for investment and consumption has increased – for example because firms are more optimistic about profits and so want to invest more. With an unchanged LM curve but a higher IS curve, interest rates would rise but so too would total income.

These conclusions about income and interest rates hold good only if the IS and LM curves have the slopes that figure 2.3 has given them. If either were vertical, different conclusions would apply. With a vertical LM curve, it would be pointless for governments to try to boost demand by cutting taxes; they would succeed only in raising interest rates. Similarly, if the IS curve were vertical, any increase in the real money supply would lower interest rates but not affect total demand.

Later chapters will develop these ideas. For now, concentrate on one aspect of the IS–LM model: the assumption that prices are stable. This assumption can now be relaxed; it is still premature to replace it with the realities of inflation, but a one-off change in prices is an instructive way to start moving in that direction.

This chapter has already shown that total demand increases when the real money supply expands. That is the same as saying that total demand increases when (a) prices fall while (b) the nominal money supply stays constant. So it is possible to link prices and aggregate demand to produce a demand curve for the whole economy.

The curve can be derived from the IS–LM model. Starting in the bottom half of figure 2.4, suppose that prices are at a level P_1, consistent with income of Y_1. That Y_1 runs up to the IS–LM diagram, and is itself consistent with an interest rate of R_1. The whole system is in balance at A_1, with equilibrium in both the money market and the goods market.

If prices fall to P_2, the LM_1 curve in the top half of figure 2.4 will move to the right, to LM_2. It will now intersect the IS curve at A_2, giving a new interest rate R_2 and a new level of income Y_2. In the bottom half of the figure, Y_2 and the lower price level of P_2 produce a new combination, A_2. Joining A_1 and A_2 gives the demand curve for the whole economy.

The key point to grasp is that the basic slope of the demand curve is downwards from left to right. When prices fall, the LM curve shifts to the right and interest rates fall. Lower interest

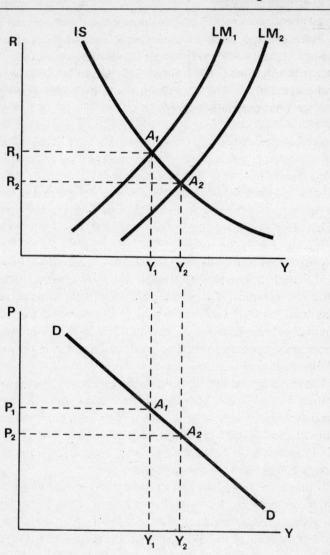

Figure 2.4

rates boost investment and consumption, so real demand rises.

Extra demand must go somewhere. This whole chapter has assumed that it goes into the eager hands of businesses which are able to supply all the goods and services demanded for investment and consumption. The next chapter will drop this assumption and see what determines supply.

3 Setting supply

The simplest model of an economy, if it is to be useful, must show how both demand and supply are determined. The previous chapter looked at demand, assuming that whatever was demanded could be supplied. This chapter tests that assumption by setting out a basic model of the economy's supply side.

In the standard textbook model of the economy, total demand rises as prices fall – the aggregate-demand curve is downward-sloping. This is not because people want to buy more goods at lower prices, in the way that they demand more bananas as the price of bananas falls. It is because a lower price level raises the real value of the money supply, which in turn leads to lower interest rates and then to higher spending on consumer goods and investment.

Economic theorists have only recently started to give as much attention to the corresponding link between prices and total supply. Their supply-side models focus on three relationships: the demand for labour as the wage rate varies; the supply of labour as the wage rate varies; and a production function which shows how much output is produced by a given level of employment. Take each in turn.

The demand for labour

Start by assuming, implausibly, that prices do not change. Also assume that the capital stock is fixed – plausible in the short-term. Profit-maximizing firms will take on extra workers until the cost of the marginal worker (for simplicity, the wage rate) exceeds the extra revenue that can be obtained from the extra output he produces.

With a fixed capital stock, the first worker that a firm employs
will easily pass the profit test. But gradually, at a given wage, a
point will be reached where extra workers cannot raise output
enough to cover their wages. Employment will therefore rise to
that point, but no further.

What happens if the wage rate falls? The cost of the marginal
worker will now be less than, rather than equal to, the revenues
he can earn, so he will be taken on. Lower wages make it profitable to employ more workers; by the same token, higher wages
make it profitable to sack some. So the demand for labour rises
as the wage rate falls.

This relationship is shown graphically in figure 3.1. As the
wage rate (W) falls, the number of workers (N) which firms want
to employ rises. So the demand for labour can be represented by
the line LD: the demand curve for labour is downward-sloping.

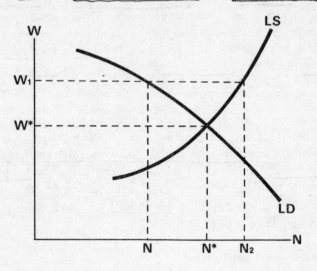

Figure 3.1

The supply of labour

In the basic model, changes in labour supply can take two forms. First, people can give up their jobs altogether (or, conversely, leave the pool of unemployed to take up a new job). Second, existing workers can raise (or reduce) the number of hours they work.

Higher wage rates unambiguously increase the supply of labour via the first route. Some people who were not previously willing to give up their leisure in order to work will be tempted by the wage rise. Similarly, a cut in wages will lead some people to stop work voluntarily, reducing the supply of labour.

The effect of a change in wage rates through the second channel is not so clear. Higher wages mean an increase in the effective cost of leisure time: if leisure is a good like any other, a rise in its price ought to mean that people want to consume less of it, and, therefore, work more. But higher wages mean that, without working any harder, people with jobs are better off. They might want to 'spend' some of their higher income by working less and 'consuming' more leisure.

In theory, the net result of these so-called 'substitution' and 'income' effects is uncertain. But in practice, adding together the individual responses of workers throughout the economy, higher wages are almost certain to raise the overall supply of labour. So the supply curve for labour will be upward-sloping, like LS in figure 3.1. The effect of high incomes on the demand for leisure may reduce the rate at which the supply of labour grows if wages rise to high levels. This accounts for the curved shape of the LS line. It takes ever bigger wage rises to keep adding to the labour supply. (If the income effect outweighed the substitution effect, the curve would not just get steeper, it would start bending back on itself.)

The labour market is in balance where the demand and supply curves cross. Figure 3.1 shows why. If, for example, the wage rate was w_1, firms would demand (according to the LD curve) N_1 workers. But N_2 workers (according to the LS curve) would want jobs at that wage, creating an excess supply of labour. That excess, in this model, drives the wage rate down; eventually, it falls to w*, eliminating the surplus of would-be workers. With a wage rate of w* and N* workers employed, the labour market is in equilibrium.

The production function

How much output do these workers produce? That will depend on both the quantity and the quality of the economy's stock of capital. The model assumes that both are fixed – the economy's physical assets are effectively frozen at a single point in time. Thanks to this simplification, the relationship between the number of workers (N) and total output (Y) – the production function – can be drawn as in figure 3.2.

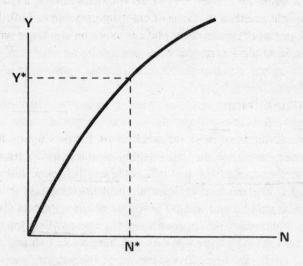

Figure 3.2

As the number of workers rises, the output produced from the fixed capital stock goes up, too. When N is low, there is plenty of capital for each new worker, so extra workers can increase output substantially; but when N is high, capital is relatively scarce, so additions to the labour force raise output by less. This application of the law of diminishing returns explains why the curve in figure 3.2 flattens off.

Note that this basic model, by assumption, lacks any theory of technological change, and therefore has nothing to say about one obviously important issue – economic growth, the subject of chapter 12. That is a flaw, but not a fatal one, so long as the model is used to explain only the short-term behaviour of the key economic variables. The way an economy develops over the longer term – what makes some countries rich, and others poor – is another matter altogether.

So labour-market demand and supply fix the number of jobs; the production function then translates that into goods and services. But how does this supply vary when the price level changes? In other words, what does the economy's supply curve look like? This is perhaps the most important, and most controversial, question in modern economics.

Let prices rise

A change in the price level has no effect on the production function, which simply describes a technical relationship between output and factors of production. But changing prices will have some effect on both labour demand and labour supply.

The next chapter will discuss how changes in aggregate supply and aggregate demand interact to change prices; for the time being, assume that higher prices just happen. What will then happen to the demand for labour? At a given wage rate (in money, not real, terms) firms will find that their marginal workers now increase revenues by more than they cost to employ, instead of merely breaking even as they did before. Firms will therefore demand more labour.

The whole demand curve for labour shifts to the right (as in figure 3.3) because, whatever the opening wage rate, higher prices mean that firms want more workers. With an unchanged labour-supply curve, the number of workers demanded rises from N_1 to N_2, exceeding the number who want to work at the wage rate w_1. Firms must attract the workers they need by bidding wage rates up to w_2, where balance is restored. The new balance will be due partly to the rise in wage rates and partly to the increase in employment.

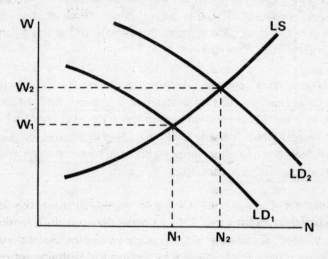

Figure 3.3

As before, the increase in employment raises output through the production function. Figure 3.4 shows what this implies for the aggregate supply curve. With prices at P_1, employment was N_1, and output Y_1. As prices rise to P_2, they raise employment by shifting the demand for labour, and this in turn raises the level of total output. So the aggregate-supply curve is upward-sloping.

But what about the effect of higher prices on the supply of labour? Figures 3.3 and 3.4 assume that the LS curve does not shift when prices rise. But if workers decide how much labour to supply on the basis of a trade-off between leisure and consumption, then higher prices – by reducing the real value of their money wage – should lead them to supply less

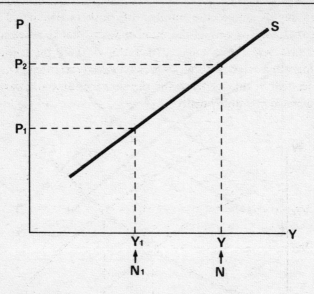

Figure 3.4

labour. As a result, the LS curve would <u>shift to the left</u>.

Figure 3.3 confirms that if the LS curve <u>does not</u> shift, workers supply <u>more labour after a price rise</u> *even though the real wage has fallen*. Prices have gone up by the vertical distance between LD_1 and LD_2 but money wages by less, from w_1 to w_2.

If workers were fully informed about price rises in the economy as a whole – and able to act on the information – the LS curve would <u>shift to the left</u>, as in figure 3.5, <u>when prices rose</u>. The labour market would then find its new equilibrium at exactly the same level of employment and *real* wages as before – money wages having risen from w_1 to w_2, just enough to offset the rise in prices.

This makes the aggregate supply curve look quite different. The rise in prices from P_1 to P_2 has done a lot of curve shifting in the labour market; but if the workers who supply labour take as much notice of price changes as the firms which demand it, those movements cancel each other out. The level of employment (deter-mined in figure 3.5) does not change, so the level of output is

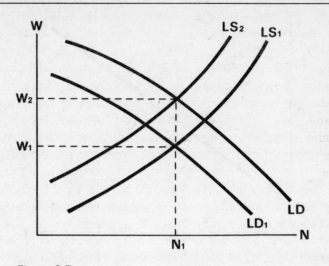

Figure 3.5

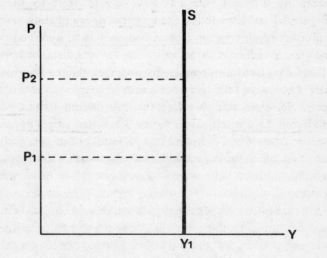

Figure 3.6

unchanged, too. Hence the aggregate-supply curve is vertical (figure 3.6).

That vertical supply curve fixes the level of employment (at N_1 in figure 3.5), but not necessarily at 'full employment' – an idea this chapter has so far left undefined. Even the version of the model that lets employment fluctuate (as in figure 3.3) gives no reason why it should settle at a level we might call full employment. In fact, both versions implicitly assume that any unemployment above the minimum consistent with people switching jobs – frictional unemployment – is voluntary. So in both cases the model can settle at what might seem a high level of unemployment and stay there, in equilibrium, simply because workers and firms are happy with that outcome.

Most economists find this unrealistic. However, it is easy to change the model so that it accounts for people who want, but cannot find, a job at the going wage rate. Suppose that wages are prevented from falling, perhaps by trade union power, by minimum-wage legislation, by over-generous social welfare systems or by deeply entrenched notions of pay comparability and fair play. Whatever the reason, if wages are held above their equilibrium level, workers will wish to supply more labour than firms want to hire.

If the wage barrier is fixed in money terms, the theory provides a case for government action to raise aggregate demand (and prices). For that would lower the wage barrier in real terms, allow the real wage to fall, and reduce the excess supply of labour. Firms would demand more workers and some of the unemployed would switch from being unwillingly out-of-work to out-of-work by choice.

That argument has a flaw: since the oil-price shocks of the 1970s, most people have become well used to reckoning with inflation. As a result, most wage rigidities, whether fixed by unions, governments or by force of habit, take account of price changes. Attempts to erode the barriers with inflation would therefore do nothing to cut real wages, and hence nothing to cut involuntary unemployment. The barriers must be taken down by other means.

Keynesian optimism, classical gloom

Many textbooks call the supply side modelled in figures 3.3 and
3.4 'Keynesian' and the supply side of figures 3.5 and 3.6 'classical'. The next chapter will make it easier to see why these labels
fit, but it is already clear why it matters so much to know which
model is closer to the real world.

The upward-sloping curve of figure 3.4 gives the government a
chance to raise employment and output by raising demand and,
therefore, prices. That might move the economy from a point like
Y_1 to a point like Y_2 without tampering with the supply-side
structure of the economy.

However, the vertical curve of figure 3.6 immediately rules out
any attempt to raise employment and output by managing
demand and prices. Whatever the price level, supply cannot budge
from Y_1. The only way to raise output is to shift the supply curve
itself, either by changing the way the labour market works, or by
altering the production function and increasing output per man.

Many Keynesians reject figures 3.3 and 3.4 as an interpretation
of their master's thought, together with the idea that governments
can raise employment only by conning workers into accepting
real wage cuts. But, at least in the short-term, this is one way that
Keynesianism does work. The issue turns on whether firms adjust
to changing prices faster than their workers.

Firms may be more closely in touch with real wages than
workers. The employer is particularly concerned about the 'product wage' – the money wage deflated by changes in the prices of
his own products. He can often forecast this quite accurately
months ahead.

Workers, on the other hand, have to predict changes in a
widely-based basket of prices, such as the retail price index in
Britain or the consumer price index in America. That is more
difficult. If their forecasts are based on past experience, a sudden
increase in inflation may catch them out, and leave them for a
time in a position like that in figure 3.3.

Another factor which may speed the adjustment of labour

demand is that firms can vary their prices frequently to match market conditions. Workers, on the other hand, are typically bound into longer-term contracts which delay compensating changes in wage rates until the next round of pay talks.

Again, this may mean that the labour-supply curve gets stuck for a time, as in figure 3.3. Labour contracts, in theory, can restore 'Keynesian' properties to otherwise 'classical' models. (Chapter 8 will look more closely at this currently active area of economic research.)

Most mainstream economists favour a compromise between the two extreme views of workers' ability to adapt to price changes: perfect flexibility versus total rigidity. In the short-term, say up to two years, they argue that the aggregate-supply curve is upward-sloping, as in figure 3.4. Workers cannot adjust to price changes as quickly as their employers because, over that sort of period, labour contracts may limit their room for manoeuvre.

But after each change in prices, the aggregate-supply curve begins to shift upwards towards the vertical. Forecasting errors are corrected, contracts and other rigidities unwind. In the long-term – arguments rage over how long is long – the supply curve will be the one shown in figure 3.6.

The next chapter concludes the review of the basic macro-economic model by bringing together the theories of aggregate demand and supply. That will show how the model determines prices – so far they have moved only by assumption.

4 Supply, meet demand

So far we have looked separately at the two halves of the economy – demand and supply. This chapter joins them up to create a simple model of the whole economy.

Chapter 2 derived the economy's downward-sloping demand curve by assuming that prices change, and tracing the effects in the markets for money and goods. Chapter 3 then derived the upward-sloping (or, as some economists would argue, vertical) aggregate-supply curve, again by assuming that prices change, and tracing the effects in the labour market.

This chapter puts these halves together, to see why prices change, and how the economy reaches an equilibrium where output demanded equals output supplied. Throughout, it assumes a closed economy. Since the advanced industrial countries are now more open to international trade – and to the effects of foreign governments' economic policies – than ever before, an important gap will remain. (Chapters 10 and 11 will try to close it.) But this simple model is a good starting-point for intelligent discussion of economic policy, and a base from which to explore newer theories.

Figure 4.1 shows a conventional aggregate-demand curve and two aggregate-supply curves. The s_k line represents the 'Keynesian' model of the labour market. In that model, workers react to changing prices more slowly than firms – perhaps because workers make mistakes in judging the level of real wages, or because they are bound by labour contracts, or because of other labour-market rigidities.

The s_c line represents the 'classical' model, in which workers have perfect foresight, and the labour market adjusts instantly to

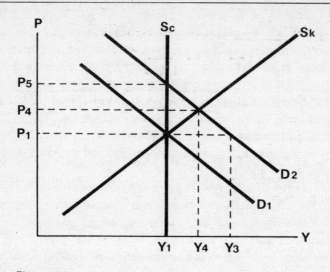

Figure 4.1

changing prices. Alternatively, think of s_k as a short-term relationship, and s_c as its long-term counterpart.

Suppose the economy is in an initial equilibrium, with output
demanded matching output supplied, with prices equal to P_1 and
output equal to Y_1. What happens if the government tries to raise
output by boosting demand, shifting the demand curve out from
D_1 to D_2?

Figure 4.1 says that, after a series of adjustments in the goods,
money and labour markets, the economy moves to a new short-
term, or 'Keynesian', equilibrium. Prices rise to P_4 and output to
Y_4. Then, in due course, the economy would drift to a new long-
term, or 'classical', equilibrium. Prices would rise further, to P_5,
and output would fall back to its original level. So the model says
that attempts to raise output through demand-management are
eventually doomed to failure. Sounds familiar?

The demand and supply curves summarize a great deal of
activity behind the scenes in the markets for goods, money and
labour. To get to grips with the model, it is worth the effort to

follow the story of the previous paragraph, step by step, using the IS–LM and labour-market models sketched in earlier chapters. (Remember that the IS and LM curves, which define combinations of interest rates and income, cross at the point where both the goods market and the market for money are in equilibrium.)

First, how is the government to boost demand? One way would be to increase public spending. That would, at least in the first instance, raise the total level of spending in the economy. So, step one is an increase in government spending, and step two, higher demand in the goods market.

This is shown in figure 4.2 as a shift in the IS curve from IS_1 to IS_2. In the initial goods-and-money-market equilibrium, the interest rate was equal to R_1, and output demanded was equal to Y_1 (corresponding to Y_1 in figure 4.1). But, with the interest rate at R_1, the extra spending would be enough to push demand to Y_2.

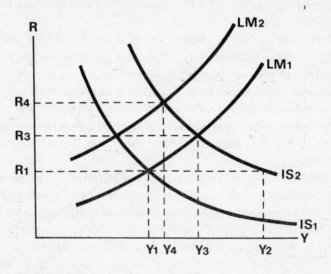

Figure 4.2

Even if prices did not start to rise, higher interest rates would immediately start to cut the extra demand; at R_1, the speculative demand for money is now too high to make room for the higher transactions demand corresponding to Y_2. The interest rate must rise to R_3, and demand fall back to Y_3, to balance the goods and money markets.

The Y_3 in figure 4.2 is the same as the Y_3 in figure 4.1. Figure 4.1 shows that the partial equilibrium on the demand side cannot last, because total supply in the economy is still less than total demand. So prices begin to rise, narrowing the gap. As the economy moves up the D_2 curve to its new short-term equilibrium at P_4 and Y_4, further adjustments are taking place in the sub-models for demand and supply.

In the goods and money markets of figure 4.2, higher prices reduce the real value of the money supply, squeezing both speculative and transactions balances again. The LM curve shifts from LM_1 to LM_2, pushing the interest rate to R_4. As a result, firms spend less on investment and the demand for output moves further up the IS_2 curve to Y_4 – the short-term equilibrium level of output.

Meanwhile, in the labour market of figure 4.3, higher prices

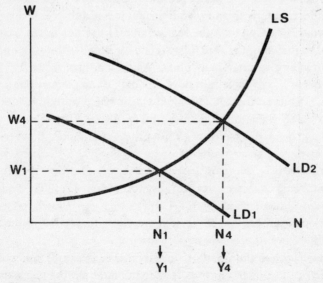

Figure 4.3

reduce the real wage, so firms increase their demand for labour. The LD curve in figure 4.3 shifts to the right, from LD_1 to LD_2, pushing the number of workers with jobs from N_1 to N_4. More workers mean more output supplied. So the gap between the initial output of Y_1 and the output of Y_4 necessary for short-term balance of demand and supply begins to close on the supply side too.

Pause at this point to ask how the new Keynesian equilibrium compares with the starting-point. Balance in all markets is restored when prices rise to P_4 (see figure 4.1), and output to Y_4. So the increase in government spending has succeeded in increasing output only at the cost of a higher price level. In the goods and money markets (figure 4.2), the interest rate has risen from R_1 to R_4. So the extra volume of demand from the initial fiscal boost has been partly offset by a fall in investment.

In the labour market (figure 4.3), the new equilibrium provides more jobs than the old. The wage rate, at W_4, is higher than before, but only in money terms. The real wage has fallen because the rise in prices is bigger than the rise in money wages.

Unfortunately, this new equilibrium is not durable. It depends on workers acting as if the real wage rate has not fallen – either because they don't realize it has fallen, or because they are unable or unwilling to alter their plans. As they adjust, however, they will begin to cut their supply of labour. So the LS curve in figure 4.3 will shift to the left. Nominal wages rise until real wages are restored to their initial equilibrium position. Employment falls back, and so does output. This process underlies the vertical supply curve, s_c, in figure 4.1.

Prices must rise again to balance supply and demand as the labour market sheds its extra jobs, and output falls. That means further adjustment in figures 4.2 and 4.3 – not shown, to spare your eyesight. The LM curve in figure 4.2 shifts further to the left, so that it eventually crosses IS, above Y_1.

In the labour market, the demand for labour rises again because of the price rise from P_4 to P_5, so the LD curve shifts further to the right. But now it is outstripped by the leftward shift of the LS curve. Eventually, LS and LD must cross above Y_1, at a nominal wage rate which leaves real wages, taking account of the rise in prices to P_5, unchanged.

So much for demand-management. The increase in public spending has raised prices without raising output. In the long-term equilibrium, lower investment exactly offsets the fiscal boost to total spending.

Figure 4.2 shows how. Investment was entirely 'crowded-out' by three doses of higher interest rates. First, the interest rate went from R_1 to R_3, because of increased demand for money; then, as prices began to move up, the real value of money balances fell, prompting the rise from R_3 to R_4; finally, the labour market adjusted, and a further round of price increases pushed the interest rate to a still higher level, consistent with the closing (and opening) level of output, Y_1.

What if the government tries to boost demand by expanding the money supply instead? Luckily, only one extra chart will give the answer. Total supply and total demand behave as in figure 4.1 – exactly the same as after an increase in government spending. Ditto the labour market.

But the story changes in the goods and money markets. Figure 4.4 shows that an increase in the money supply shifts the LM curve to the right, from LM_1 to LM_2. At the initial interest rate, R_1, there is now enough money to finance a demand for goods of Y_2. But the actual demand for goods, given by the IS curve, is still only Y_1. Because of this excess money supply, the interest rate starts to fall. That narrows the excess supply of money in two ways. First, the speculative demand for money rises as the opportunity cost of holding it falls; second, the transactions demand for money rises as lower interest rates increase investment and consumption.

The goods and money markets reach a partial equilibrium at Y_3 (corresponding, as before, to Y_3 in figure 4.1). But now there is an excess total demand for goods, so prices start to rise, to P_4 in figure 4.1. The real value of the money supply falls, so the LM curve shifts back from LM_2 to LM_3 (figure 4.4). The interest rate

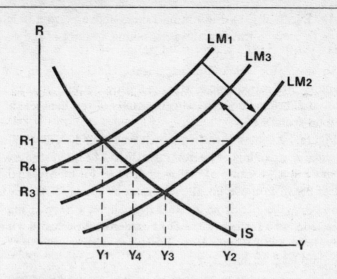

Figure 4.4

moves back up from R_3 to R_4, output demanded falls to Y_4, and, on the demand side, the economy arrives at the 'Keynesian' equilibrium of figure 4.1.

Forces in the labour market (see figure 4.3) simultaneously move the supply of goods to the new short-term equilibrium. As in the case of a fiscal boost, employment rises to N_4, and output to Y_4, as prices rise to P_4. The only difference between the resting-place after a monetary boost and an equivalent fiscal boost is that interest rates are lower in the case of monetary expansion. As a result, output will be balanced in favour of higher (private-sector) investment and lower (public- or private-sector) consumption.

The transition to long-term, or classical, equilibrium is just as before. As the labour market gradually adjusts to the first rise in prices, the LS curve in figure 4.3 begins to shift to the left. Employment falls back towards its original level, and therefore so does output. That creates excess demand in the economy (figure 4.1), so prices must rise further, to P_5. That cuts the real money supply for a second time, so the LM curve in figure 4.4 shifts back to its original position, restoring interest rates and output demanded to their opening levels. Eventually, all the major economic variables are back at their starting points – except prices.

What is monetarism?

Originally the argument between Keynesians and monetarists was about the proper roles for monetary and fiscal policy. Keynesians favoured fiscal policy (taxes and government spending) as a way of influencing aggregate demand; monetarists preferred monetary policy (interest rates and the money supply). Why? One (disputed) interpretation casts the answer neatly in the IS–LM mould.

Keynes's original analysis of a recession or slump emphasized the risk that, at very low interest rates, people may not care whether they hold money or bonds. That would put the economy

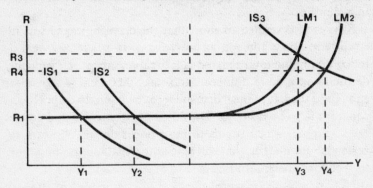

Figure 4.5

in a 'liquidity trap', as in the left-hand side of figure 4.5. Because the LM curve is flat, changes in the money supply, which shift LM, will have little effect on output demanded. A cut in taxes, on the other hand, by shifting IS along the flat LM curve, would increase demand from Y_1 to Y_2.

Monetarists concentrated on a different case. If interest rates are very high, speculative demand for money is squeezed to almost zero, so that the LM curve (see right-hand side of figure 4.5) is almost vertical. Hey presto, a tax-cutting shift in IS will have relatively little effect on aggregate demand, while a money-expanding shift in LM will raise demand from Y_3 to Y_4.

The early dispute between Keynesians and monetarists therefore seemed to boil down to nothing more complicated than an argument over the slope of the LM curve. An obvious compromise was to admit that both theories made sense: use monetary policy to dampen demand if interest rates soar (e.g. in a boom), and fiscal policy to stimulate demand when interest rates are low (e.g. in a slump).

Keynes also wanted to show that the classical model was inconsistent. His argument, again recast in IS–LM terms, went as follows. Suppose total demand falls because, say, people suddenly decide to save more. Suppose, too, that the IS curve moves far enough to the left to push demand into the liquidity trap. How is equilibrium to be restored? The fall in aggregate demand creates excess supply, which begins to push prices down. With a Keynesian labour market, that will reduce aggregate supply and bring the economy back into balance.

Not so, says the classical model. Lower prices, it insists, can only feed through to output by shifting the LM curve. But, say Keynesians, this will have no effect if the LM curve is horizontal. The economy will stay stuck in depression, refuting the classical economists' view that it will always right itself after being knocked off-course.

The liquidity-trap debate is dead. Now most so-called monetarists believe that demand-management can affect output and employment only briefly, while Keynesians argue that the effects may last longer. So the focus of the argument has shifted to the supply side of the model. The central question is how the labour market reacts to changes in total demand. Economists are still obsessed with slopes. But now it is the slope of the aggregate-supply curve they care about.

Unstable inflation

The model of aggregate demand and aggregate supply is a static model; it compares one stable economic equilibrium with another. As a result, it is suitable for analysing only a single change in the price level, and not a process of continuously rising prices – inflation. An inflationary economy is never stable. Demand and supply curves are in perpetual motion.

Fully dynamic models, though complicated, alter few of the static-case conclusions. For example, in the static Keynesian model, cutting unemployment requires a once-for-all rise in prices; in the corresponding dynamic model, cutting unemployment requires a rise in the inflation rate. The analogy goes further. If price expectations in the labour market adjust immediately, and workers are free to respond, the static model says that employment cannot increase as the price level rises. In the corresponding dynamic model, if inflation expectations in the labour market adjust immediately, with workers free to react, unemployment cannot be reduced by increasing the inflation rate.

The simple static framework – now somewhat old-fashioned – is only a starting-point for discussing economic policy. The following chapters will describe more recent elaborations. Some reject the idea that there is any period during which demand management may be effective, arguing that the aggregate-supply curve is vertical even in the short run. Others say that the period between the 'Keynesian' and 'classical' equilibria is long enough to make demand management worthwhile.

5 Expecting the future

Economists have always agreed that the future affects the present, but have never been sure in what ways. They have spent a lot of time trying to define expectations about the future and then feeding them back to current behaviour. A new theory suggests that the feedback is fast and has far-reaching implications. Known as the rational-expectations approach, it has forced Keynesians and monetarists alike to reassess their views.

Economists now agree that even the simplest economic theory has to say something about how people view the future. They have tried to develop ways of defining and measuring expectations. These efforts are relatively new: Keynes in his *General Theory* had treated expectations as exogenous, because he doubted that they could be modelled or measured accurately.

The simplifying assumption of exogenous expectations produces, for example, the basic consumption function described in chapter 2: consumption in a particular period is influenced by income in the same period. But any assumption that lifetime or 'permanent' income determines consumption begs the question of how people gauge their likely future income.

Economists have provided various answers, largely based on the principle that expectations of the future are formed by experience of the past. The two earliest versions of this idea were:

Extrapolative expectations

If interest rates rise from year to year in the sequence 4 per cent, 6 per cent, 9 per cent, people will expect them to rise next year. Some may simply extrapolate the absolute increase – two percentage points from 4 per cent to 6 per cent, three points from 6 per cent to 9 per cent – and conclude that next year's rate will be four points higher at 13 per cent. Others might look at the rate of change – a 50 per cent rise from 4 per cent to 6 per cent and then from 6 per cent to 9 per cent – and guess that next year's jump will be up to 13.5 per cent. Either way, they are looking at the direction of past movements and saying that it will continue.

Most theories of extrapolative expectations put greater store by the recent than the distant past. In the 1970s, many people in a country like Britain could remember that inflation had run at only a few per cent a year in the 1950s and 1960s, so they did not exclude the possibility of it doing so again. But they were much more influenced by their recent experience of double-digit inflation, and thought that was more likely to continue.

Adaptive expectations

Extrapolation suggests that people observe the past as a way of predicting the future. But the theory does not let them learn from their own mistakes, so some economists refined it. They suggested that people do use their own forecasting errors to derive their next forecasts.

That seems quite plausible. If you have lost money on Knacker's Nag in each of its past five races, you will probably avoid it in the sixth. You may not choose Lucky Lady, who wins by a distance, but at least you will have avoided your earlier mistake.

Adaptive and extrapolative expectations are not all that different: it is possible to show mathematically that an adaptive expectations rule is equivalent to a particular kind of extrapolative expectation. Both theories have an obvious weakness. They say that the future performance of a particular variable is affected only by its past. If Lucky Lady has never raced before, neither theory would provide any reason for backing her. Yet her past form, or lack of it, is not the only factor that will dictate her future.

Punters might be influenced by her pedigree, for example, or the success of other horses from the same stock. People trying to predict even a single variable will take account of dozens of other factors, if they think them relevant. That piece of common sense led economists to construct a wider theory of expectations.

The new theory is called 'rational expectations'. It first appeared in the economic literature in 1961, but has been a major theme only since the mid-1970s. Like much else that is new in macro-economics, rational expectations has strong microeconomic roots. It is based on a familiar microeconomic idea: people are rational in the sense that they do the best they can. As consumers, workers and investors, they watch all the market's signals.

The theory of rational expectations says that people form their views of the future by taking account of all available information, including their understanding of how the economy works. If they are trying to predict next year's inflation rate and are of mone-tarist bent, they will look at last year's growth in the money supply. Those who think that prices depend on costs will look at wages, productivity, commodity prices etc., plus (perhaps) the pronouncements of O.P.E.C. oil ministers.

Rational man

Many economists initially rejected the rational-expectations approach, mainly because it seemed to demolish Keynesian econ-omics. More recent work has shown that it does not. But some economists still challenge the theory on its merits as a plausible description of reality. They say that people without degrees in mathematical economics cannot and do not sift through all the information available on the economy, and out of that chaos produce a rational forecast of, say, inflation.

That is not necessary, reply the supporters of rational ex-pectations. The economic forecasting industry is thriving and its results are widely reported, even in the popular press. But fore-casters can never agree, the critics might reply. Some are Key-nesians, some monetarists – they cannot all be right, and their

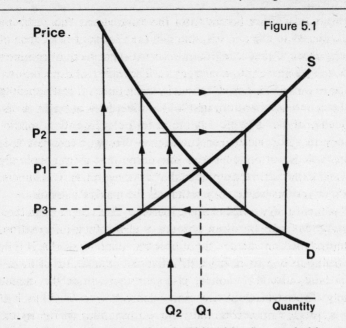

Figure 5.1

forecasts cannot all be rational. This objection probably over-states the disagreement between forecasts – more than one or two years ahead, they usually cluster around consensus figures. More importantly, individuals can differ from one another in their ex-pectations and still be rational if they are using different in-formation. But when all these individual expectations are added together, errors tend to cancel out – producing an aggregate view of the future that reflects all the available information. (This is known in the jargon as the law of large numbers.)

Furthermore, rational expectations theory does not say that people will not make mistakes; simply that they will not go on making the same kind of mistake year after year, when the in-formation they need to correct that mistake is to hand.

This defence of rational expectations has persuaded many economists. The theory has one immediate implication. The more accurate the information that people draw on, the less will the future surprise them. They have already adjusted their present behaviour to take account of it.

From this notion economists have developed the 'random-walk' theory to explain, for example, the ups and downs of share prices. Stockmarkets are full of information, runs this argument, and today's share prices embody it. They are therefore the best guide to tomorrow's prices; the only thing that will cause them to move is new information, and that is inherently unpredictable.

Such analysis has a gloomy moral for people wanting to make money in stockmarkets or currencies: they won't, unless they have inside information about something that will happen and will move the market in a predictable way once it becomes known. For everybody else, the opportunities for making a profit are so fleeting that they do not really exist. This gives rise to a rational-expectations joke about an economics professor walking with a keen-eyed student across the university quad. 'Look,' says the student, pointing at the ground, 'a five-pound note.' 'It can't be,' replies the rational professor. 'If it were there, somebody would have picked it up by now.'

His reply emphasizes that the information which moves markets must be really new, not something that people could anticipate. An apparently unfavourable event – a strike, a rise in interest rates – often leaves share prices unchanged. This is be-cause the markets were expecting it to happen and had already adjusted prices.

The same is true of other economic variables, say supporters of rational expectations. They do not claim that everybody possesses perfect foresight. Their assumption is more modest – that people make only random forecasting errors, not systematic errors that they go on repeating. If that is correct, the current set of prices – exchange rates, interest rates, wages, product prices, etc. – is continuously adapting to incorporate the future.

To see the implications of this theory, apply it briefly to three familiar areas.

The 'cobweb' model of consumers and producers

Most textbooks on economics include figure 5.1, which shows how some markets can move erratically from one period to the next. If the supply of potatoes is reduced by blight from Q_1 to Q_2, the market will move away from its equilibrium at P_1Q_1 to a higher price P_2. At that price, farmers will plant more potatoes but consumers will demand less. So the next harvest will push prices down to P_3, discouraging farmers from planting so much. From year to year, prices will jump about, and more so every year.

Rational-expectations theory provides an answer to this. It says that producers are able to see beyond the immediate future. Farmers realize that planting much more after a blight will only glut next year's market, driving down prices and losing them money. They will therefore head straight back to equilibrium by planting Q_1 of potatoes in the year after the blight. In other words, the cobweb model assumes a timelag in production; but rational expectations shows that it is really an information gap, which need not exist.

Inflation

If everybody believes that faster monetary growth will produce faster price inflation, they will anticipate those consequences. When the central bank starts speeding up monetary growth, savers will immediately demand higher interest rates – and borrowers will oblige, because they are prepared to pay interest rates that are the same in real terms as before the monetary expansion. The currency markets will push down the country's exchange rate (provided other countries are not also boosting their monetary growth by the same degree). Workers will demand higher wages – and employers will pay them, because they are simultaneously pushing up their prices.

In fact, everybody is acting to bring about the faster inflation that they expect. If they move instantaneously, they will prevent any of the faster monetary growth translating into higher spending in real terms, even for a moment. 'Reflation' will simply mean inflation.

Economic forecasting

Conventional forecasting models used to be based on past behaviour – a past when certain economic policies were operating.
If these policies continue, the models may give an accurate guide
to the future. But what happens if the policies change, which is
usually the question that forecasters ask of their models? The
theory of rational expectations says that the very structure of the
model will then change, so attempts to forecast the future will be
based on a now-irrelevant past. This argument, first put forward
in 1976 by Professor Robert Lucas of the University of Chicago,
casts serious doubt on the validity of forecasting. Most forecasters
have tried to answer its objections by formally including expectations in econometric equations.

Because of its significance, the rational-expectations approach
can easily be assumed to say more than it does. At this stage it
needs stressing that the theory does not stand or fall simply on
whether people make instantaneous adjustments. Adjustment has
costs – putting new prices on goods in a shop, sending new
catalogues to customers, reopening wage negotiations, writing to
your bank to switch money into a deposit account, etc. People
may correctly expect the future but still decide to delay their
response. If delay costs less than immediate adjustment, then it is
the rational thing to do.

Schools of thought

The implications of the rational-expectations approach will often
crop up in later chapters. The approach has helped to define new
boundaries between different schools of economic thought. Although sticking labels on people can mislead, here is a shorthand
description of the three main (non-Marxist) schools of modern
economic thought:

New classical

The leaders of this school are two Americans, Professors Robert Lucas and Thomas Sargent; in Britain, Professor Patrick Minford of Liverpool University is the leading light. The new classical economists believe that (a) expectations are rational and (b) markets clear very quickly. By this they mean that willing buyers and willing sellers strike bargains which leave them all happy – because wages and prices are flexible, both up and down.

This pair of assumptions means that governments cannot use a fiscal and/or monetary boost to increase output and employment. As a result, involuntary unemployment can happen only briefly and then for only one reason: because wages are fixed infrequently, workers may temporarily price themselves out of work by having wrongly guessed the equilibrium wage rate. As the rational-expectations theory says that they will not persistently make this mistake, involuntary unemployment will not persist. So unemployment tends to be at its 'natural rate'. It exists because some people choose to be unemployed – for example, because they can get a higher disposable income from unemployment pay and other state benefits than from a job.

Monetarist

The best-known monetarist is Professor Milton Friedman, long of Chicago University and now at the Hoover Institution in California; British adherents include Sir Alan Walters, who was Mrs Thatcher's economic adviser during her government's first term. Monetarists believe that economies have a natural tendency to full employment, but that this can take several years to achieve because prices and wages adjust rather slowly. Some monetarists think expectations are rational; others (including Professor Friedman) tend to see them as extrapolative or adaptive – another reason why economies may be slow to return to full-employment equilibrium.

Some old-fashioned monetarists still argue that reflation via a fiscal boost will raise interest rates but not demand, because the LM curve (in the basic IS–LM diagram described in chapter 2) is vertical. But monetarists of all vintages believe that the only lasting effect of boosts to demand (whether monetary or fiscal) will be on prices, because the long-run aggregate-supply curve is vertical. Thus they see no point in trying to fine-tune demand, and advocate a stable and slow rate of monetary growth.

New Keynesian

This term covers several Nobel prize winners: in America, Professors Laurence Klein and James Tobin; in Britain, Sir John Hicks and Professor James Meade. They also believe that economies tend to a full-employment equilibrium, but that they may take many years to reach it unless governments boost demand during a recession. This will be effective in boosting output, they say, because the short-term aggregate-supply curve slopes up from left to right. In the long-term, however, they agree with new classicals and monetarists that the supply curve is vertical, so output can be increased only by raising productivity.

New Keynesians argue that economies take so long to return to full employment because the stickiness of wages and (to a lesser extent) prices prevents markets from clearing. Some new Keynesians see this stickiness as proof that expectations are not rational; companies and workers do not learn from their errors in forecasting the levels of prices and wages that are needed to clear markets. Most new Keynesians think that expectations are rational; the snag is wages, which are so rigid – because of contracts, minimum-wage laws, trade-union power, .etc. – that they prevent some people from getting a job even though they want one.

What do these distinctions mean for puzzled finance ministers trying to steer their economies to non-inflationary growth? Popular discussion of economic policy still revolves around Keynesianism (old-style) versus monetarism (ditto). But most academic economists think that distinction is at best irrelevant, at worst misleading. They have accepted the rational-expectations approach, and incorporated it in both new classical and new Keynesian theories. This has helped to highlight the real disagreement between the two schools: whether markets clear.

6 Beefing up demand

Chapter 2 described the basic theory of demand. That now needs refining.

When theories advance, they do not necessarily become more complicated. They may simply be bringing in more of the real world, in the process becoming more familiar and accessible. In demand theory, some of the building blocks set out in chapter 2 remain unchanged. Demand is still divided into two main components, consumption and investment. And the aggregate-demand curve still slopes down from left to right, with output demanded increasing as prices fall.

Within that general framework, researchers have concentrated on explaining more accurately what it is that determines consumption and investment. Their efforts have been a mixture of the theoretical and the empirical: developing plausible theories and then testing to see whether they square with the evidence. The statistics on consumption and investment are abundant and fairly reliable. But some theories are hard to express in a way that makes them suitable for testing.

Start with consumption. The simplest model – which has consumption being determined by income – has been refined in three ways. First, by introducing other variables that affect consumption; second, by making income into a long-run notion; and third, by applying the rational-expectations approach.

New variables

Economists have long recognized that interest rates affect consumption. To take an extreme example, if interest rates were to double while everything else in the economy was unchanged, people would have a bigger incentive to save, and therefore to forgo some consumption. This suggests that people will increase their savings when real interest rates rise, but reduce them when real rates fall. That is not necessarily so: in Britain in the mid-1970s, real interest rates went negative for long periods, yet the personal savings ratio rose. In the early 1980s, by contrast, real rates were positive, while the savings ratio fell (see figure 6.1).

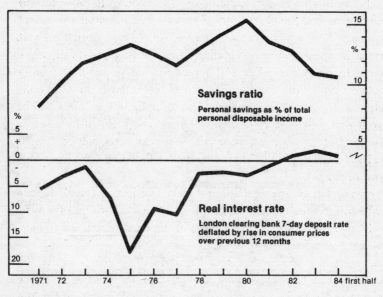

Figure 6.1

The difference between the two periods highlights the importance of inflation as an independent influence on savings and consumption. Economists therefore distinguish between (a) a wealth effect, which describes how a change in interest rates affects consumption; and (b) a real-balance effect, which shows the effects of changing prices on consumption.

To see how the wealth effect operates, suppose that the price level is constant and that interest rates fall. That increases the value of bonds and other capital assets like houses, making people feel richer. It also cuts the cost of borrowing. As a result of a fall in real interest rates, consumers spend more.

The real-balance effect can also produce an increase in consumption – but from a rise in real interest rates. To see how this perverse conclusion is reached, suppose that prices fall. The real value of people's money balances will rise. That adds directly to their wealth, even if nominal interest rates have not changed. Again, consumers will spend more.

None of this is very conclusive. So economists have started paying more attention to another way that inflation can affect consumption, which does not depend on changes in real interest rates. Suppose you have a loan of £100, with a standard arrangement to repay capital at £10 a year for ten years while paying interest on the outstanding balance. If real interest rates are constant at 5 per cent, in a world of no inflation you will pay £15 in your first year (£10 of capital, £5 of interest). But if inflation is running at 15 per cent, your real first-year costs will be £26.10 (£10 of capital, plus £20 in interest, all deflated by the 15 per cent rise in prices).

Even though the real interest rate has not changed, higher inflation means that the burden of repayment is brought forward – high repayments (in real terms) in the early years, low repayments (in real terms) at the end.

Figure 6.2 shows that this 'front loading' increases as the inflation rate rises. The faster the inflation, the more a borrower has to put aside in the early years to service his loan – so the less he has left for consumption. For the whole economy, this effect of inflation is hard to predict. Among other things, it depends on demography – on how many young people are becoming big borrowers while the middle-aged and elderly are paying off the last of their depreciating mortgages.

These different influences can help to explain the behaviour of personal savings in Britain over the past ten years. The savings ratio rose in the mid-1970s despite negative real interest rates, because inflation was raising the cost of servicing loans and also eroding the value of money balances. People hold part of their

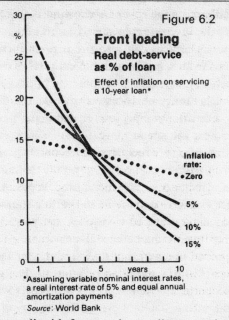

Figure 6.2

Front loading

Real debt-service as % of loan

Effect of inflation on servicing a 10-year loan*

Inflation rate:
• Zero
5%
10%
15%

*Assuming variable nominal interest rates, a real interest rate of 5% and equal annual amortization payments

Source: World Bank

savings in very liquid form – in readiness to buy consumer durables, for example, or to pay quarterly gas and electricity bills.

When these prices are rising rapidly, people may decide to increase their savings even as a proportion of their incomes. So although negative real interest rates apparently made it attractive to borrow and spend rather than save, stronger forces were at work pushing up savings.

Long-run income and consumption

Chapter 2 mentioned the permanent-income hypothesis, first proposed by Professor Milton Friedman. He argued that people's spending in any particular year does not depend on the size of their income in that year, but on what they believe will be their average annual 'permanent' income over their lifetime. If their actual income is less than their permanent income, they will borrow to make up the difference; if more, they will use the opportunity to save.

From a different angle, this approach also sheds light on the behaviour of the savings ratio in Britain and many other industrial countries. The mid-1970s were a period when people were bound to reassess their permanent incomes. Higher oil prices and higher unemployment had ended the 'age of abundance'; many people no longer believed that their real incomes were going to rise steadily year after year. If they scaled down their permanent income, they immediately reduced their consumption and started to save a larger slice of their current income.

All long-run notions of income naturally depend on people's expectations of what their income will be. Professor Friedman's original work was based on a model of adaptive expectations: people would make their best guess of their permanent income and at any one time would not expect that to change. If experience repeatedly proved them wrong, they would alter their guess.

More recent work has extended this approach to include rational expectations.

Rational expectations

This theory assumes that, on average, an individual's best guess of his permanent income is extremely good. It incorporates all relevant historical information – for example a person's career and earnings pattern so far – plus all available information about the future, such as salary scales, personal ambition and the likely path of taxation. In fact, the average person has no reason to change his views of his permanent income and therefore no reason to change his consumption. How much he spends this year is the best guide to how much he will spend next year and thereafter. Consumption is a random walk.

As with other random-walk variables, permanent income and consumption can be altered by new information. If a war breaks out, for example, people abandon (or anyway postpone) their plans to increase their incomes. Sudden sickness might have the same effect. But a lot of the humdrum information that emerges over time will not be surprising and therefore will not alter consumption.

This conclusion has significant implications for economic policy and the stability of the whole economy. All long-run models of income and consumption suggest that an individual's consumption will not change much. The easier he finds it to borrow in early life to bring his actual income up to his permanent income, the smaller the change will be. As consumption follows a stable path, and as it also accounts for about two thirds of G.N.P., the economy as a whole looks pretty stable.

However, this reassuring message depends on the kind of expectations that people have. With the adaptive expectations of the basic Friedman model, a change in actual income has to persist for some time before people recognize that their permanent income has changed. Their consumption is correspondingly slow to adjust. If somebody's actual income rises by £100 in a year, he may initially save it all – spending more only as he comes to believe that his permanent income has risen by £100. In other words, his marginal propensity to consume is initially zero; boosting his income will not produce any multiplier effect on consumer spending.

With rational expectations, the multiplier may be quite different. The person may have good reason to believe that the extra £100 will continue in future years, so he will immediately alter his estimate of his permanent income. In that case, he will spend part of the £100 in year one. With a marginal propensity to consume of more than zero, he is creating a multiplier effect on spending in the whole economy. This is in line with Keynesian models of consumer behaviour – one major example of how rational expectations, far from undermining Keynesian analysis, can actually strengthen it.

Investment ideas

Until about twenty years ago, economists used to treat investment as a flow of spending on capital goods, just as consumption was a flow of spending on consumer goods. This approach was changed to seeing investment as the difference between two stocks of capital: the amount of capital a firm actually had versus the amount it wanted.

This new perspective – 'stock adjustment', in the jargon – can be applied to other economic variables. A later chapter will use it to discuss the effects of the government's budget deficit on the rest of the economy. At this stage, note how it makes investment a simpler concept to grasp. In particular, it makes it easy to analyse investment within the conventional framework of profit-maximizing firms.

Companies will achieve their desired capital stock when the cost of buying an extra unit of capital is equal to the extra profits it will earn, with the stream of future profits being discounted by a suitable interest rate and expressed in present values. If the marginal cost of capital is less than the present discounted value of its future profits, it will pay a company to buy more capital – i.e. to invest. Note that this is net investment; there is always some gross investment going on, because companies are replacing the worn-out bits of their existing capital stock (though even then they will invest only if they think it profitable to do so).

This model makes it clear that investment will be influenced by three main variables: (a) the price of capital goods; (b) the rate of interest, because that will determine whether future profits are large enough to service a loan with which to buy more capital; and (c) the profits that are expected to be earned from investment. If a company is in equilibrium, with its actual capital stock equal to its desired stock, it will be pushed off this equilibrium only by a change in one or more of these three variables.

How quickly will it return to equilibrium – or to put it another way, how long does investment take to respond to a change in any of the three variables? Suppose that (c) changes: for exogenous reasons (such as new technology), companies become more optimistic about future profits. They will want to increase their investment. But the industry supplying capital goods cannot meet all this extra demand, so it puts up its prices. This persuades some companies to delay their investment plans until the price of capital goods falls back.

Now introduce rational expectations. Just as that approach treats consumption as being dependent on a person's lifetime income, so it gives a central role to the long-run element in investment – the present value of future profits. It also treats that value as incorporating all available information, and changing only when previously unanticipated facts crop up.

Figures 6.3 and 6.4 illustrate how investment can change in response to new information. They are based on the assumption that the price of capital goods is the variable which adjusts fastest when equilibrium is disturbed. And they start with investment in a 'steady state', when companies have the capital stock they want and are investing only for replacement.

Figure 6.3 has interest rates falling in Period T_1 without any company expecting them to. Firms then want to invest more. The prices of capital goods jump. As higher prices bring forth more supply, actual investment also jumps – from A to B. For a time, firms will be undertaking net investment as well as more replacement investment (because the capital stock is larger). The actual division between net and replacement can be established mathematically, but will follow the line AC fairly closely.

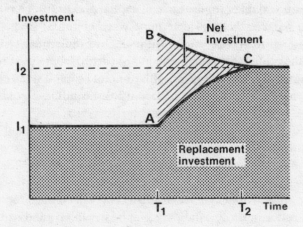

Figure 6.3

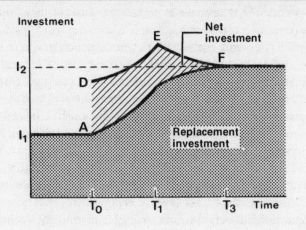

Figure 6.4

In time, firms will have done all the extra investment they wanted to and will return to the steady path of replacement investment. That new path, I_2, will of course be higher than the original one, I_1, because the capital stock has been increased and so more needs to be replaced.

Now suppose, in figure 6.4, that the fall in interest rates is not unexpected. By period T_0, companies are anticipating it even though the fall does not actually happen until T_1. They recognize that the price of capital goods will jump once the fall in interest rates occurs, so they reckon they will save money by buying early.

However, not every company buys more capital goods in T_0, for two reasons. (a) Firms do not all earn the same rate of return on an extra unit of capital; those with the highest short-run returns will have the biggest incentive to move first. (b) Some firms cannot afford to invest more until the interest rate has actually fallen. At the rate prevailing in T_0, they would not find it profitable to buy more capital goods.

The companies that get in early, before T_1, do push up the price of capital goods, but not by as much as if every company had waited for interest rates to fall. Investment in T_0 therefore rises from A to D (figure 6.4).

Between T_0 and the actual fall in interest rates in T_1, more firms decide that they can afford to buy extra capital goods because the prevailing interest rate will soon change. So investment continues to build up. Again, part of the extra spending is for replacement investment because the capital stock has increased; the line A F suggests the division between net and replacement investment.

By the time interest rates fall, investment has risen to E. Just as in figure 6.3, it then starts to subside until companies regain a steady state at the higher level of replacement investment.

In a rational-expectations analysis, investment is probably more jerky than it is in a model where firms are influenced only by the past. But it does not become a random walk as consumption does when it is given the rational-expectations treatment. The difference is that companies have got some aspect of the future that is uncertain (as opposed to being wholly known or wholly unknown, which is the case with consumers). Firms can speculate on the price of capital goods; some will invest in the belief that the price will shortly rise, others may delay in the hope of a fall.

7 What deficits do

Simple models of the economy have a significant gap. They ignore the way that the government's budget deficit creates new financial assets for the private sector to hold.

Previous chapters have discussed the role of government policy in the economy. They assumed that policymakers can freely raise public spending or cut taxes, regardless of what happens to the government's budget. A finance minister's task is not that simple.

Take the case of an increase in public spending. Provided that the government had previously matched its income and expenditure – balancing its budget – the increase in spending will create a budget deficit. That deficit has to be financed, either by adding to the money supply ('printing money') or by selling government bonds (borrowing).

The government's need to finance its deficit does not directly affect the supply side of the model developed in earlier chapters. But taking the deficit into account changes the demand side of the model in important ways. Recent theories have extended the IS–LM framework to show how.

In figure 7.1 the demand side of the economy is initially in equilibrium, with interest rates at R_1 and output demanded at Y_1. Assume that the budget deficit is zero at that point. If the government now raises public spending, the IS curve shifts from IS_1 to IS_2, and output demanded rises to Y_2. But higher public spending means that the government now has a budget deficit. If it finances that deficit by creating money, the LM curve will shift from LM_1 to LM_2, boosting demand still further.

The LM curve will carry on shifting to the right as long as the budget deficit persists and the government chooses to finance it

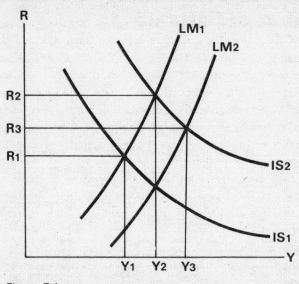

Figure 7.1

by printing money. But two factors will gradually slow this process, and bring the economy to rest at a new equilibrium.

First, the increase in demand raises prices, reduces the real value of the money supply, and so brakes the LM curve's move to the right. This inflationary process – as the aggregate-demand curve shifts up the aggregate-supply curve – was described in detail in chapter 4. Recall that with a Keynesian aggregate-supply curve, the demand boost will raise both output and prices. In the classical case, only prices will rise.

Second, if extra demand does bring forth extra output, this will reduce the budget deficit by increasing tax revenues. As the LM curve shifts, the budget deficit is falling; eventually, even if prices did not rise, the economy would reach a new level of output at which the budget deficit was cut to zero. The money supply would no longer need to increase; the economy would be back in equilibrium.

On one interpretation, the simple IS–LM model implicitly assumes that the government covers its deficit not by printing money, but by selling bonds. That is why interest rates rise when the IS curve shifts to the right – higher interest rates are the incentive for people to hold more bonds. But that cannot be the end of the story, because if people are buying bonds they are increasing their wealth. The stock of financial assets is growing, so the economy cannot be in equilibrium.

What will be the effect of this growing stock of government bonds? If the private sector feels wealthier, it may spend more on goods. A bond-financed budget deficit will therefore shift the IS curve further to the right than the simple model supposed, giving a bigger increase in demand.

At first sight, it seems like double-counting to claim an extra boost from fiscal policy on the grounds that bond-financing makes people wealthier. If people have lent their money to the government to pay for public spending, how can they spend it themselves as well?

Imagine an economy (still with no international trade) where the government has no income and no demand for goods and services; the private sector has an income of £100. It spends £70 of this on its own output, and saves – i.e. spends on investment goods – £30. The government then decides to spend £10, and borrows from the private sector to finance it.

Government spending feeds straight through to the private sector, so its income rises to £110. It will probably save the same proportion of its income as before – £33, of which £10 will be spent on the new government bonds. The rest, £23, will be spent on investment goods. This is less than before, because the government has had to let interest rates rise to make its bonds attractive to the public, squeezing out some private investment.

In the next period, suppose government spending falls back to zero. What will happen to consumption? It will be higher, says the wealth-effects theory, because the private sector now has some financial assets in the shape of its £10 of government bonds. Consumers feel richer, so from now on they will spend, say, 71 per cent of their income on consumption, and only 29 per cent on investment goods. That increase in the propensity to consume shifts their IS curve to the right.

The theory that a bond-financed deficit makes the private sector richer may be arithmetically sound. But Professor Robert Barro of Chicago University argues that it is economically false. He has led the revival of an idea first mooted by the nineteenth-century English economist, David Ricardo; hence his ideas have been labelled 'neo-Ricardian'.

The Barro argument, much in keeping with the new classical approach to economics, goes as follows. When the government sells bonds to finance its spending, people realize that it will have to service (and eventually repay) its borrowing. The only certain source of government revenue is taxes, so extra borrowing will in time mean higher taxes. The private sector does not treat its bond purchases as increased wealth, but as a portent of increased taxes. To prepare for that day, people reduce their consumption and increase their savings by the whole amount of the increase in government spending.

As a result, not only is there no wealth effect in consumption; there is also no expansion of demand through the familiar multiplier process. The effect of an increase in public spending financed by bond sales is exactly the same as if the government had financed its extra spending by raising taxes immediately and keeping its budget balanced.

What if the deficit is financed by printing money? A similar argument applies, according to Professor Barro. The rational man in the street will realize that printing money will in time increase inflation. That, in turn, will reduce the real value of his money holdings. He therefore decides to save more to maintain his real cash balances, so his consumption immediately falls below what it would otherwise have been.

Until Professor Barro's contribution, the obvious counter-argument to these neo-Ricardian views was to argue that a tax deferred is the next best thing to a tax not levied. If today's consumers know that a budget deficit will raise taxes paid by future generations, they have no reason to increase their own saving. So a budget deficit will have multiplier effects in the short-run, and Keynesian demand management can be effective.

Not so, argued Professor Barro. If households care about succeeding generations, they have effectively infinite time horizons. Parents who know that their children will have to face higher taxes in the future because of an increase in the budget deficit today start saving more immediately so as to leave their children a bigger bequest. They will cut their consumption and cancel out the expansionary effects of the deficit.

This theory, like much of the debate about new classical economics, seems to divide economists into those who think it obviously true and those who think it too preposterous for words. One critic, Professor James Tobin of Yale University, managed to take the idea seriously just long enough to write down some objections.

Here are two of the most important.

First, some households are childless, and not all parents care about what their children's tax bills will be when they have grown up and are earning their own incomes. People such as these will spend more today at the expense of future generations if their taxes are lowered and governments rely on borrowing instead.

Second, even if people lived to infinity, they would probably wish to bring their spending forward in time. Living standards rise with economic growth; most children are better off than their parents were. Today's consumers may welcome budget deficits as a way of doing what would otherwise be rather difficult – accepting gifts from future generations. If so, a higher budget deficit will not prompt higher savings, and its boost to total spending will not be offset.

The debate about whether deficits create wealth shows no signs of cooling. But suppose (a) that a bond-financed budget deficit does increase private-sector wealth, and (b) that higher wealth does shift the IS curve to the right. Figure 7.2 shows how the initial fiscal boost pushes the IS curve from IS_1 to IS_2; then the wealth effect takes over, pushing the curve to IS_3 or beyond.

The same factors which ensured that rising demand from a money-financed deficit is first slowed and then stopped will do the same in the bond-financed case.

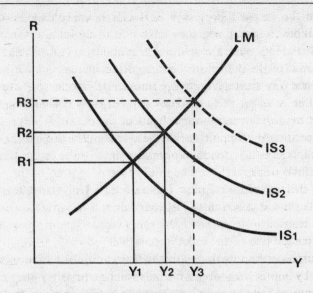

Figure 7.2

First, rising demand means excess demand in the economy as a whole, which puts upward pressure on prices. Higher prices reduce the real value of the money supply and shift the LM curve to the left. So the effect on income of the IS curve shifting to the right is at least partly offset by the LM curve moving to the left. Higher prices also slow the shifting IS curve directly, by reducing the real value of the wealth which bond-financing creates.

Second, as the IS curve shifts to the right, the budget deficit is falling, because higher output means higher tax revenues. So, even without an increase in prices, the economy will eventually come to rest at a level of output where the deficit is wiped out, and stocks of financial assets in the economy are no longer changing. Figure 7.2 shows how the IS curve shifts first from Y_1 to a short-term equilibrium at Y_2, and then drifts out slowly to a long-term equilibrium at Y_3, where the higher level of output is assumed to bring in enough taxes to cut the budget deficit to zero.

So far, the stability of this model is not in doubt. The effect of a bond-financed increase in public spending is more effective than the simple theory says, and the economy still reaches an equilibrium in due course.

But what if there are wealth effects in the LM curve? Traditional theories of the demand for money stress the need for money to finance transactions; they give little weight to the role of money as a store of wealth. The newest theories, however, emphasize that money is just another financial asset, albeit with special properties. This implies that, as people increase their wealth, they also increase their demand for money, in order to keep a balanced portfolio of assets.

If this 'portfolio-balance' approach is correct, the wealth effect shifts the LM curve to the left over time. Figure 7.3 shows why this may mean trouble for the supposed self-righting properties of economic models. If, because of rising wealth through extra government bonds, the budget deficit shifts the LM curve to the left by more than it shifts the IS curve to the right, output demanded falls from its short-term equilibrium of Y_2 to a new position at Y_3.

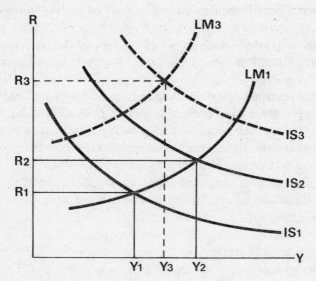

Figure 7.3

At this lower level of output, the budget deficit is bigger than at Y_2, because of smaller tax revenues. The IS and LM curves must shift again, reducing output still further, raising the deficit – and so on, indefinitely. This pattern of adjustment leads to a continued growth in the budget deficit; the economy moves further and further away from an equilibrium where the stock of financial assets is constant.

As with wealth effects in the IS curve, changing prices may brake or reverse this process. As output falls, prices are pushed down. That will boost the real value of the money supply, and try to shift the LM curve in figure 7.3 back to the right. But there is still no guarantee, in principle, that the net effect of these forces will not be an ever-accelerating fall in output.

In practice, economies do not show this catastrophic instability. But it is important to know that stability cannot be deduced from theory. And the model highlights the crucial role played by flexible prices in trying to restore equilibrium. If declining output does not succeed in pushing down prices, then the economy is even more likely to be unstable.

Measuring up

In recent years public discussion of economic policy has centred on budget deficits – not because they pose a risk of fundamental disequilibrium, but because of their crowding-out effects on investment and interest rates. President Reagan's critics say America's budget deficit is too big; Mrs Thatcher's say Britain's is too small. But what do 'big' and 'small' mean? Economists try to adjust the actual figures of the deficit in two ways:

Cyclical adjustment

Imagine an economy in which the government does not alter its policies through the course of the business cycle. In practice, that will mean a large deficit in slumps and a small deficit (perhaps a

surplus) in booms. In an economic slowdown, higher unemployment will boost the public sector's spending on social
benefits, without any decision to be more generous to the jobless.
The recession will also cut revenues automatically, because taxes
will be lower than they would otherwise have been. Conversely,
when the economy booms, government spending falls and its
revenues rise.

This suggests that changes in the deficit come from two sources:
first, automatic changes from the economy's position in the business cycle, known as the cyclical deficit; second, changes due to
government policy – the structural deficit. Calculating the two
components can be a hit-and-miss affair. The usual method is to
use a large model to simulate the state of the economy at full
employment. The difference between the full-employment deficit
and the actual deficit measures the cyclical element. Changes in
the full-employment deficit itself are equivalent to changes in the
structural deficit.

The trouble is that these estimates depend heavily on which
model you choose. Broad-brush models like the one developed in
this book are hopelessly inadequate because they do not show
how economic activity affects particular tax and revenue programmes. But detailed models often disagree about the way the
economy works. More fundamentally, does the split between
cyclical and structural really say anything useful? The whole deficit has to be financed, and both components place upward
pressure on interest rates. The structural deficit shows how much
of it can be blamed on changing policy, but that does not mean
that the cyclical deficit is economically insignificant.

Inflation adjustment

Taking inflation into account does suggest a reason to concentrate on one part of the deficit. Governments spend money not
just to buy goods and services. They must also pay interest on the
national debt. In turn, this interest can be split into a real rate of
return and an amount to compensate bond holders for inflation.
Many economists say that the right deficit to watch and control

is the nominal deficit less the inflation component in debt interest. They argue that what matters is the change in the real value of outstanding debt. Algebra can show that the inflation-adjusted deficit (the nominal deficit less the inflation component in interest payments) is exactly that. If governments set the inflation-adjusted deficit to equal zero, the real value of debt outstanding would be held constant. The nominal deficit, of course, would be equal each year to the inflation component – roughly, the inflation rate multiplied by the value of outstanding debt.

This means that, in an economy with inflation, balancing the nominal budget is a more restrictive policy than it first seems. For example, if governments are concerned about the pressure which their borrowing places on interest rates, the right indicator of that pressure is the real value of debt. When inflation is high, the real value of a fixed nominal amount of government bonds is falling. So high inflation may raise the (nominal) demand for new bonds, and governments will be able to borrow more without pushing interest rates up.

8 Extending supply

Chapter 3 discussed the basic theory of aggregate supply. This chapter looks at some applications and further developments of the supply-side approach.

It is no accident that economists paid less attention to the theory of demand and more to the theory of supply during the 1970s. Two massive increases in the price of oil confronted them with a puzzle. The oil shocks were sure to have big effects, but the preoccupation with aggregate demand made it hard to see what they might be. Economics needed supply-side theories to show how shocks like this could explain 'stagflation' – high unemployment combined with high inflation.

For simplicity, take the case of Factoria, an industrial country with no oil of its own. Dearer oil affects it in two separate ways. First, Factoria will use less oil, so that (in the short term, at least) a given amount of labour will be able to produce less final output. This effect is equivalent to a downward shift in the production function of figure 8.1.

Second, because oil is more expensive, the revenue produced by each extra worker in Factoria's firms will be reduced. So the marginal product of labour falls, which is equivalent to shifting the labour-demand curve from LD_1 to LD_2 in figure 8.2. Together, these changes cut output first from Y_1 in figure 8.1 to Y_2 and then to Y_3, and the number of workers employed from N_1 to N_3.

This assumes that the overall level of prices has not changed. Figure 8.3 shows that the combination of lower output (Y_3) and constant prices (P_1) corresponds to a shift in the aggregate-supply curve from S_1 to S_2.

The next step is familiar from chapter 4. At P_1, there is excess

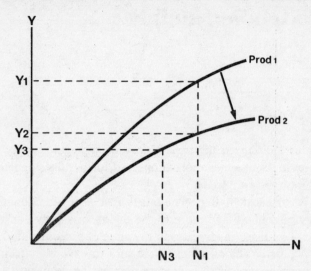

Figure 8.1

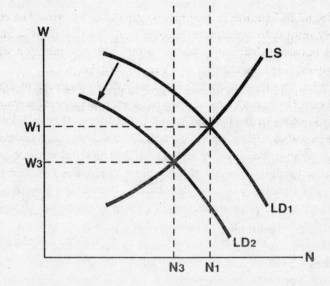

Figure 8.2

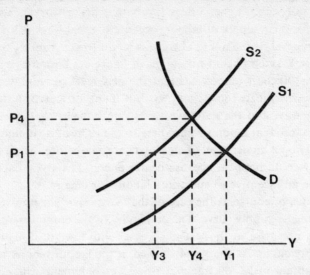

Figure 8.3

demand in Factoria's economy, so prices start to rise. The economy returns to equilibrium only at P_4Y_4. So the oil-price shock has boosted prices and reduced output – the combination which demand-side analysis was at a loss to explain.

What about the workers? The theoretical apparatus of figures 8.1 to 8.3 does not give a clear-cut answer to the question whether employment in Factoria falls as a result of an oil-price hike. To see this, look at figure 8.1. Figure 8.3 shows that output comes to rest somewhere between Y_1 and Y_3. But if it turned out to be above Y_2, that would imply a level of employment greater than N_1, the opening position. Because the production function has shifted down, employment might be higher even though output has fallen.

The solution to this paradox lies in figure 8.2. As chapter 4 explained, the labour market adjusts to a new equilibrium at a higher price level through shifts in the demand and supply curves for labour. Higher prices make firms want to hire more workers at the going wage rate because the marginal product of labour has gone up. Higher prices (probably) make workers want to reduce their supply of labour, because the real wage is lower for every level of the nominal wage rate. So to get from Y_3 to Y_4 in figure 8.3, the LS and LD curves of figure 8.2 both move up.

The likeliest outcome is that the new level of employment is somewhere between N_3 and N_1. But if the LD curve shifts up a long way, and the LS curve shifts only a little, the new curves might cross at a point somewhere to the right of N_1 in figure 8.2, implying a higher level of employment than before the oil shock. That could happen, because dearer energy has given Factoria's firms an incentive to substitute labour for energy.

This, of course, is the case of the 'Keynesian', or non-vertical, aggregate-supply curve. The ambiguity of the employment effect does not arise in the 'classical' case, with a vertical aggregate-supply curve. As chapter 4 showed, if the labour market adjusts instantaneously to changing prices, employment will not rise above N_3 in figure 8.2, the level to which it drops soon after the oil shock. From that point, LS and LD curves rise together, holding real wages constant as prices rise from P_1 in figure 8.3.

Most economists agree that the classical model gives a truer picture than the Keynesian model of the long-term state of the economy. This is depressing: can it really be true that an increase in the relative price of an essential import like oil will *permanently* raise the level of unemployment? Yes, unless workers are willing to work as hard as they did before, and for lower real wages.

Such a change of attitudes would shift the aggregate-supply curve (in both 'Keynesian' and 'classical' models) back to the right, restoring unemployment. But a narrow theory of labour supply, which thinks of individuals trading off income against leisure, can come up with no reason why attitudes should change. When real wages fall, so will the supply of labour. If this theory is correct, it helps to explain the stagflation of the 1970s.

Son of Phillips curve

So far this book has used a type of economic analysis called comparative statics. This method assumes that economic shocks (a change in government policy, a change in oil prices, etc.) move the economy from one stable position to another. In practice, however, economies are never at rest. In the jargon, they are 'dynamic'. Much of the most difficult modern theory explores this dynamism. A simpler strand has refurbished an old statistical relationship – the Phillips curve – in a way that sheds further light on the economy's supply side.

The original and familiar Phillips curve was drawn in an article in 1958. It plotted inflation (strictly, changes in wage rates) against unemployment and found that when inflation was high, unemployment was low and vice versa. The relationship seemed to hold good for many years and in different countries. It seemed to suggest that a government could choose to cut unemployment by tolerating a slightly higher rate of inflation.

By the late 1960s, that happy relationship was breaking down. The Phillips curve seemed to shift upwards over time, so that a particular level of unemployment corresponded to ever-higher inflation rates. How do economic theorists account for this?

In a dynamic economy, wages and prices can both be increasing at constant levels of output, employment and real wages. In effect, the aggregate-demand and aggregate-supply curves are moving up together over time. If the economy is growing, output and real wages can also be rising continuously. If the growth rate of output was 3 per cent a year, prices might rise at 5 per cent a year and wages at 8 per cent a year, all at a constant level of employment.

The crucial idea behind the theoretical Phillips curve is that the rate of increase in wages (and prices) will depend on the degree of slack in the labour market. If the excess supply of labour is high, it will have a strong dampening effect on the wage–price spiral; but excess demand for labour will accelerate the wage–price spiral. This is a new element in the economic model described in this book: the *level* of unemployment (taken as a measure of excess labour supply) is assumed to have an effect on the *rate* at which wages (and prices) change.

However, expectations of future price increases also affect the rate at which wages change. If, at some given level of unemployment, workers expect prices to rise by 10 per cent, they will raise their wage demand to 10 per cent above what it was before. This changes the Phillips curve dramatically.

Figure 8.4 shows a short-run Phillips curve (SRPC) and a long-run Phillips curve (LRPC). Suppose the economy is at point A on the short-run curve and the government decides to expand demand to reduce the unemployment rate from u_1 to u_2, at point B. Lower unemployment means less slack in the labour market and hence the rate of wage inflation rises from wi_1 to wi_2.

But in due course, the cost-push pressure of wage inflation also increases the rate of price inflation. That feeds back into wage demands and pushes the rate of wage inflation up again, to wi_3 at point C. Joining points A and C gives the long-run curve, which offers policymakers a less attractive trade-off between jobs and prices. Some economists argue that the long-run curve is vertical, in which case the trade-off disappears entirely.

Even this long-run relationship depends on a timelag between changing prices and changing wages. The theory says that in the short run none of the change in prices brought about by the initial policy stimulus feeds through to wage demands, and that in the long run only part of it feeds through, because workers never adjust their wage demands fully.

Enter rational expectations. If workers correctly anticipate the inflationary effects of the government's attempt to cut unemployment, the whole of the increase in prices will immediately be added to wage demands. That will prevent any slowdown in the growth of real wages – the precondition for creating new jobs.

So if (a) expectations are rational, and (b) firms and workers respond immediately to their new expectations, the Phillips curve is vertical, even in the short run. The government cannot push unemployment below u_1 in figure 8.4 simply by allowing inflation to rise above WI_1. As in other examples discussed in chapter 5, the effect of rational expectations, in markets which clear, is to collapse a long-drawn-out adjustment into a single moment, rendering useless any policies which rely on timelags for their effectiveness.

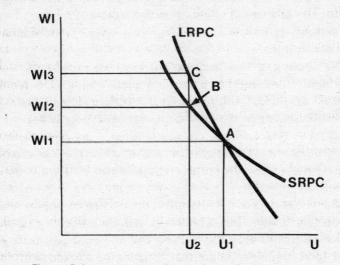

Figure 8.4

There is a clear link between this 'expectations-augmented Phillips curve', as the theorists call it, and the classical model of aggregate supply. Both imply that unemployment has a 'natural' rate; any attempt to drive it below that rate by boosting demand will succeed only in boosting inflation. Hence the natural rate sometimes goes by another name – the non-accelerating inflation rate of unemployment, or N.A.I.R.U.

These theories do not say that the N.A.I.R.U. is fixed, so questions which ask how there can be a 'natural' rate of unemployment when the actual rate fluctuates so widely are beside the point. Supply-side shocks can shift the aggregate-supply curve, raising or lowering the N.A.I.R.U.; so can changes in the work-versus-leisure preferences of workers.

A different question is harder for these theories to answer, and provides a stronger case for governments to try to manage demand. Why do firms in many countries prefer to reduce their wage bill during a recession by cutting their workforces rather than by cutting wages (or the rate of wage increases)?

During the 1970s, many economists tried to explain how wages (and prices in general) might be sticky because of implicit contracts between buyers and sellers. Two broad labour-market theories emerged.

The first argues that firms do not regard the unemployed as perfect substitutes for the workers they already employ, nor recent recruits as perfect substitutes for experienced staff. Senior workers acquire specific skills which would be costly for their employers to find among the unemployed. This gives them a degree of monopoly power within the firm, which they can exploit to raise wage rates above the revenue earned by the marginal (new) worker.

Where that happens, it will affect the pattern of employment not only in recession but in booms as well. Even when the labour market is tightening, firms will be able to avoid paying large wage increases. They know that their senior workers will not want to quit to join other firms – because if they did, they would be new workers, and so would lose the premium pay that they can extract from their current employers.

'Fair play' then demands that experienced workers are protected from falling real wages. As a result, firms can save money on their wage bill in a recession only by sacking their least experienced workers. Most firms do operate this kind of last-in-first-out policy for lay-offs – strong evidence that an implicit contract with senior workers leads firms to vary employment rather than wage rates.

According to the second theory, firms like taking risks more than workers do. Entrepreneurs, by their nature, are risk-takers. Moreover, they have good access to capital markets which allows them to hedge their risks if they choose. Neither is true of workers. Profit-maximizing firms can try to exploit this difference by offering their workers a remuneration package which is, in effect, part wage and part insurance service: workers will accept lower average pay if firms protect them from variability in pay. Firms, as a result, have a clear incentive to make wages sticky.

The benefit to workers, however, is less obvious. Firms must still react to changing demand for their goods. If they hold wage rates steady, they will sometimes have to vary the size of their workforces instead, and the workers who are sacked in slumps will face a more extreme variation in their pay than they bargained for. Why, then, should workers prefer fixed pay with a relatively high chance of unemployment to variable pay with a relatively low chance of unemployment?

If workers received no income when they became unemployed they would choose indifferently between a variable-wage 'contract', and a fixed-wage 'contract' with a slightly higher chance of unemployment – the benefit of a low-risk fixed wage cancels out the higher risk of the sack. But workers do receive income during unemployment, in the form of state welfare benefits. That shifts the balance in favour of the fixed-wage deal. The result is bigger fluctuations in employment during the cycle.

Laffer's free lunch

To some, 'supply-side economics' is much easier than this chapter has made it seem. For them it stands for a single idea – a government can cut taxes and reduce its budget deficit at the same time. The argument is simple: lower taxes mean bigger incentives, hence higher output; that will widen the tax base enough to increase overall tax revenues, even though tax rates are lower. Professor Arthur Laffer, once adviser to President Reagan, is the most celebrated supply-sider. His Laffer curve (see figure 8.5) shows that as tax rates rise beyond a certain point, T^*, the disincentive to work cuts output by so much that tax revenues fall. With taxes of 100 per cent, nobody works at all, so revenues are zero.

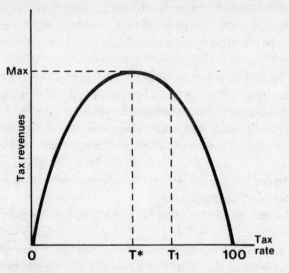

Figure 8.5

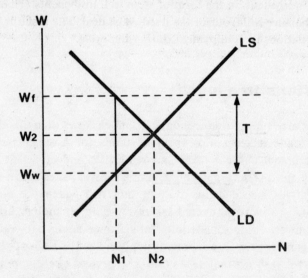

Figure 8.6

The idea that a tax cut can raise output and employment is not revolutionary. Keynesians, for example, would agree. The controversial part of Professor Laffer's idea is that output and employment can rise without any deficit-induced increase in aggregate demand. Figure 8.6 shows how this might come about through changes in the labour market. Suppose that an income tax equal to T separates the wage paid by firms, w_f, and the wage received by workers, w_w. If the tax was abolished altogether, the wage rate (paid and received) would move to w_2, and employment would rise from N_1 to N_2. In effect, the aggregate-supply curve for the whole economy would shift to the right, raising output and lowering prices.

Would the rise in output be enough to outweigh the lower rate of tax and cut the budget deficit? If taxes were abolished, revenues would fall to zero and a budget deficit would remain. The deficit will fall only if T is cut from a point, like T_1, to the right of T^*. Most economists agree that taxes in industrial countries are well to the left of T^*. Cutting them may still be a good way of raising output and employment. But those who see lower taxes as a way of improving the government's finances may have to learn to love $200 billion budget deficits.

9 When markets jam

So far we have described a model which has been cast in the IS–LM mould. Some economists think that this framework distorts Keynes's economic thinking. They suggest a different interpretation, based on what happens to markets when prices are sticky.

The IS–LM diagram still dominates the economics textbooks almost fifty years after Sir John Hicks first used it to summarize Keynes's *General Theory*. Its virtues are obvious: by bringing together information about complex behaviour in two separate markets (the market for goods and the market for money), it shows how events in one can affect the other.

Many of the developments in economic theory since Keynes, discussed in previous chapters, can be seen as attempts to flesh out the bare IS–LM bones. Adding a labour market to the model meant that the demand-side analysis of IS–LM could be combined with a theory of supply, to give an explanation of changes in prices and employment. Adding wealth effects to the IS and LM curves removed an implicit inconsistency in the model, and showed that in some circumstances it might be unstable. Chapter 11 will fill the model's biggest gap by adding international trade.

Few of these advances were seen at the time, and least of all by the economists responsible for them, as mere additions to IS–LM. The theorist's natural wish to overturn prevailing orthodoxy was not the only reason for that. Like most syntheses, IS–LM could embrace new ideas only by simplifying them, shaving off the idiosyncratic corners which, their discoverers believed, contained what was novel and significant. Though most economists are happy to take the IS–LM diagram as a starting point, different factions within the monetarist and modern-Keynesian groupings reject it out of hand.

Sir John Hicks himself has pressed one important objection to IS–LM. The model is one in which, for the most part, markets clear. Remember that the IS and LM curves state the conditions necessary for equilibrium in the goods and money markets, and implicitly assume that these conditions will hold.

According to the IS–LM framework, interest rates (and, if the model is supplemented with a supply side, prices) will move to ensure that markets clear, avoiding any danger of lasting excess demand or supply. The price of money (the interest rate) and the price of goods are the channels through which events in one market affect the other. In a sense, they provide the essential information which markets need if they are to clear.

But does IS–LM analysis really assume that all markets clear? Previous chapters used the model to discuss theories of un-employment – 'excess supply in the labour market'. In fact, the model provides a good explanation for voluntary unemployment: that real wages are too high to let employment rise to some desired level. But if unemployment is voluntary, the labour market is clearing. There is no excess supply of labour, because everybody who wants work at the going wage can get it.

The IS–LM model can explain involuntary unemployment only by assuming that wages (unlike other prices) are rigid. As a result, it regards large-scale unemployment – the phenomenon which Keynes set out to explain – as a special case of the classical economy. If Keynes's *General Theory* boils down simply to the classical model plus an arbitrary assumption of wage rigidity, it hardly stands as a revolution in economic thought.

This observation gave rise to a strand of economic research which has tried to reinterpret Keynes's thought. According to one view, what Keynes really cared about in the *General Theory* was the role of prices as signals of the state of markets. He doubted that prices could effectively carry information from market to market and thereby ensure equilibrium. If this is right, what could be more absurd than to force his theory into a frame-work which takes perfect price flexibility for granted, and allows for wage rigidity only as some sort of special case?

The new theorists wanted to know how an economy would behave on the extreme assumption that prices are completely inflexible. Such an assumption is no use for analysing the long-term changes in an economy, but over a short period it fits parts of the real world quite well. Firms, for example, do not change their prices and wages every day. They have to respond to changing market conditions in other ways – by adding to or reducing their stocks, and by hiring or firing workers.

If quantities change

How can markets interact without the mediation of smoothly changing prices? In the early 1970s, Professors Robert Barro of Chicago University and Herschel Grossman of Brown University developed a model to answer that question. They brought to-gether an analysis of the labour market by Professor Don Patinkin of the Hebrew University of Jerusalem and an analysis of the goods market by Professor Robert Clower of Northwestern University. Their idea was to show that disequilibrium in one market could reinforce disequilibrium in the other.

Figure 9.1 shows goods on the vertical axis and labour on the horizontal axis. If prices and wages were flexible, they would move to clear both markets. Suppose that in such an equilibrium households supplied L_1 of labour and demanded G_1 of goods, as at point H.

This point shows the goods that households want to buy and the labour that they want to supply at existing prices and wages. Economists call these amounts the households' notional demand for goods and notional supply of labour. When markets clear, as at H, the households' wishes are satisfied, and their notional demand and supply become effective demand and supply. But if markets fail to clear, that disequilibrium may force a gap between the notional and the effective.

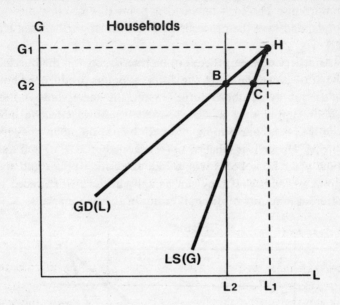

Figure 9.1

Now suppose that for some reason firms only demand L_2 of labour. If prices and wages are fixed, there will be an excess supply of labour, equal to the distance between L_2 and L_1. As a result, households will jointly have lower incomes and will therefore demand fewer goods, say G_2 at point B.

As the vertical line above L_2 is moved leftwards across the chart from point H it will trace out the households' demand-for-goods curve. Except at point H, it shows effective rather than notional demand. Another way to describe this demand is to say that it is influenced by rationing in the labour market. Hence the curve is labelled GD(L) – the demand for goods with labour rationed.

What if households faced a different kind of rationing? Suppose that for some reason the supply of goods were limited to G_2, so that households could not satisfy their notional demand for G_1 of goods. If they reduced their labour supply all the way to L_2 they could still afford to buy G_2. But they would most likely not reduce their labour supply that much. They can make a compromise choice – move to a point like C, consume G_2 of goods, and save the proceeds of the extra labour between B and C.

Another curve can therefore be traced; moving the horizontal line at G_2 down the chart, the different points produce the households' supply-of-labour curve. Again, the curve shows notional labour supply only at H; elsewhere it shows effective labour supply, or labour supply reduced by rationing in the goods market. Hence it is labelled LS(G). Together, GD(L) and LS(G) show what households would like at existing prices and wages (point H), and what they can actually achieve when faced with different amounts of disequilibrium in the two markets.

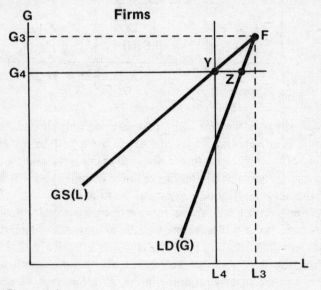

Figure 9.2

Figure 9.2 repeats the process for firms. Point F shows firms' notional demand for labour (L_3) and notional supply of goods (G_3). If households supply less labour than firms want at the going wage, firms will be able to supply fewer goods. The firms' effective supply-of-goods curve, GS(L), is traced out by moving the line above L_4 to the left.

Firms may also be unable to sell all they would wish. That means they will employ fewer workers. If the limit on sales is G_4 in figure 9.2, for example, they will produce at a point like z, using the extra production from the labour between y and z to add to their stocks. Moving the horizontal line at G_4 down the chart produces the firms' effective labour-demand curve, LD(G).

Just as the IS–LM framework shows involuntary unemployment as a special case, these so-called 'wedge diagrams' can be used to show the market-clearing equilibrium as a special case. Figure 9.3 puts the households' wedge together with the firms' wedge.

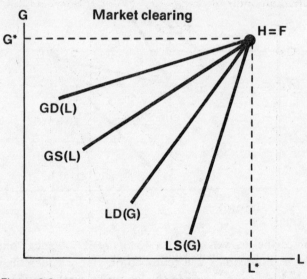

Figure 9.3

The precise slopes of the four effective-demand and effective-supply curves will vary according to the model's assumptions. One big question is how far households (and firms) prefer to consume (and produce) today rather than in the future; that will affect the distance between B and C in figure 9.1 (and the distance between Y and Z in figure 9.2). More important, though, is whether the wedges come together, as in figure 9.3, at the same point

(H = F). When they do, firms and households can all achieve their notional demands and supplies – for L* of labour and G* of goods. Everybody is happy.

Not so in figure 9.4. In this case, firms want to sell more goods than households want to buy, and buy less labour than households want to supply. So F is to the north-west of H. What will be the amounts of goods and labour traded, if prices cannot change?

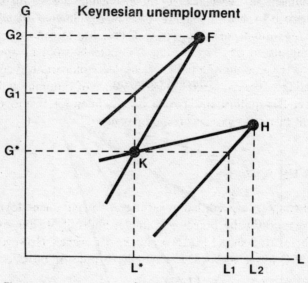

Figure 9.4

To see the answer, go back to figure 9.1. Under voluntary exchange, households will refuse to buy more goods than they want (subject to rationing in the labour market) – so they reject any point above the GD(L) line. Similarly, they will refuse to sell more labour than they choose (subject to rationing in the goods market) – so they reject any point below the LS(G) line.

Voluntary exchange, however, is quite consistent with households buying fewer goods than they would like, if firms will not sell enough. It is consistent, too, with them supplying less labour than they would like, if firms will not hire enough. So households will accept points on or between the two lines of the wedge.

The same argument applies to firms – they will reject points outside their wedge of figure 9.2. Now return to figure 9.4. The closest firms and households can get to their first-choice positions (F and H respectively), without moving outside their wedges, is K. That means G^* of goods traded and L^* of labour traded – much worse than you might have guessed from the original disparity between F and H.

L^* implies two levels of involuntary unemployment. First, the difference between L^* and L_1, which is the amount of labour which households want to supply if they are forced to restrict consumption to G^*. Second, the difference between L_1 and L_2, which is the amount of labour which households want to supply at existing prices and wages, in the absence of rationing in both markets. Disequilibrium theorists usually lump the two together and call them 'Keynesian unemployment'.

Finding a cure

Earlier chapters argued that governments can cut unemployment only temporarily by boosting demand, and only to the extent that the extra demand leads to cuts in real wages. However, in figure 9.4, lower real wages might have little or no effect on jobs.

Lower costs would make firms want to increase output and hire more workers, so F would shift upwards and to the right. But pay cuts would make households want to work less and reduce their spending, shifting H downwards and to the left. K might stay put: employment would stick at L^*. True, as H moves, L_2 would fall towards L^*, trimming unemployment a little. But excess supply in the goods market would increase as F moves.

The real solution to the unemployment of this model is the traditional Keynesian remedy of extra aggregate demand – not surprising, since the model shows excess supply in both markets. A tax cut would raise households' notional demand for goods, moving H upwards, and pushing K towards F. An increase in public spending would narrow the gap in another way. F shows the goods which firms want to supply to the private sector. If the government spent more, there would be less left over for private consumers. So excess supply in the goods market would be cut, and employment would rise, as F fell towards H.

Figure 9.4 shows one pattern of disequilibrium. Other patterns can cause involuntary unemployment which is immune to extra demand. For example, it turns out that the unemployment of figure 9.5 is best cured by lower real wages – the classical remedy. In this case households want to buy more goods than firms want to sell, and supply more labour than firms want to buy. So instead of excess supply of both goods and labour (the 'Keynesian' case), the diagram shows excess supply of labour combined with excess demand for goods.

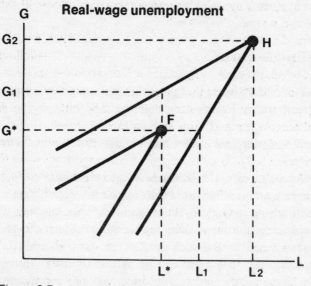

Figure 9.5

The labour-market outcome of figure 9.5 is quite similar to the Keynesian case. Households want to supply L_1 of labour, given the constraint of G^* on what they can buy. In the absence of goods rationing, they would want to supply L_2 at existing prices and wages. So the difference between L_2 and L^* is involuntary unemployment.

But now households would like to buy more than firms are willing to sell, even though they have got far fewer jobs than they want. With jobs rationed at L^*, households would like to buy G_1 of goods; if jobs were freely available, they would want to buy G_2 of goods. Firms are only willing to trade G^*.

In the Keynesian case, households are rationed once – in the jobs market. They can adjust their demand for goods, and buy what they want subject to that constraint. In the case of figure 9.5, they are rationed twice. They cannot demand or supply what they want in either market. Reflecting that distinction, firms are rationed once in the Keynesian case – in the goods market. But in figure 9.5, they are not rationed at all – goods and labour are traded at F, the point which firms would freely choose at existing prices and wages.

Extra demand, which moves H up in both diagrams, would make the disequilibrium of figure 9.5 worse. Unemployment would be unaffected while the excess demand in the goods market increased. But lower real wages would shift F upwards and to the right, and H downwards and to the left. So cuts in real wages would narrow the gap from both sides.

Note one other difference between figure 9.4 and figure 9.5. Where there is real-wage unemployment, households want to buy more than they can get. In the longer-term, that will bid prices higher and reduce the excess demand for goods. This model should eventually start to act in a market-clearing way. In the Keynesian case, firms are building up stocks, but no faster than they want to, given the restriction of G^* on goods traded. They have no reason to cut prices and reduce the excess supply of goods. This model could stay in disequilibrium permanently.

Professor Barro, one of the pioneers of the disequilibrium approach, has since disowned it. Far from advocating models which assume that prices are sticky, he is now a leader of the new classical school, and argues for market-clearing theories.

According to the new classical economists, it is wrong simply to assume that prices are sticky; economic theory must explain how prices can stick if firms and households behave rationally. (The previous chapter gave one answer – implicit contracts between buyers and sellers.) Modern Keynesians can reply that theory seems as much at odds with the evidence when it assumes that markets clear quickly and smoothly. Perhaps the best way to judge the debate is to think of the disequilibrium models as pictures of the economy in the very short term, and models with price flexibility as a better guide to changes in the long run.

10 Why exchange rates change

The switch from fixed to floating exchange rates in the early 1970s prompted economists to new theorizing and research. Although none of their work offers a get-rich-quick guide for currency speculators, it helps to show why exchange rates move.

The Bretton Woods conference of 1944 established a system of fixed exchange rates. Not fixed forever, though; when a country was in 'fundamental disequilibrium' on its balance of payments, it could and should change its exchange rate. For example, Britain devalued sterling in 1949 (from $4.03 to $2.80) and again in 1967 (to $2.40). And even a fixed rate was allowed to fluctuate within a band of 1 per cent on either side of its parity.

The architects of Bretton Woods intended exchange rates to change very seldom. If a change were needed, its timing and size should be uncertain (to stop speculators making a killing) but its direction should be predictable. If country A's inflation was faster than its trading partners', it devalued its currency; if slower, it revalued. Country A would then bring its costs back into line with the international norm, and so would no longer trade at an unfair disadvantage or advantage.

This approach to exchange rates gave a central role to international trade. It assumed that a country's exchange rate was mainly the price at which it bought imports and sold exports, and that adjusting this price would alter how much of each it bought and sold. Capital flows – the money that one economy attracted from others or lent to the rest of the world – were deemed only marginal. At the time that was a reasonable view. For more than twenty years after the Second World War, most governments tightly controlled the international movement of capital.

The emphasis on trade and the price of tradeable goods and services has produced one theory of exchange rate behaviour. It is called purchasing power parity (P.P.P.) – shorthand for the idea that exchange rates will tend towards the point at which the international purchasing power of currencies is equal. Since inflation erodes a currency's purchasing power, the difference between inflation rates in two countries will determine how far one currency erodes in terms of the other – i.e. how their exchange rate moves.

Suppose countries X and Y have equal purchasing power in year one and no inflation. In year two, inflation jumps to 10 per cent in country X. According to P.P.P., country X's exchange rate would in time depreciate by 10 per cent. This is sometimes expressed as the idea that 'real exchange rates' – nominal rates adjusted for differential inflation – are constant.

The P.P.P. theory raises two awkward questions.

First, which is the base year when purchasing powers were equal? In practice, there is no starting point of zero inflation and equilibrium exchange rates from which all subsequent movements can be judged. The choice of a base year must therefore be arbitrary – and can make a big difference to the conclusions of P.P.P. analysis. Take the dollar as an example. With a base year of 1979, its real exchange rate in mid-1984 had appreciated (i.e. the competitiveness of American producers had deteriorated) by 36 per cent. Using 1982 as a base, the rise in the dollar's real rate by mid-1984 was only 9 per cent.

Second, how should 'inflation' be measured in different countries? For analysing changes in relative costs, it makes no sense to use indexes of consumer prices. They include things like housing costs, which are not part of international trade, and indirect taxes which change domestic prices but not international ones. Wholesale prices have fewer of these drawbacks, but again cover items that are not internationally traded.

Those who favour P.P.P. to explain currency movements therefore tend to choose a measure of competitiveness which covers manufactured goods alone, because they are all tradeable. And

Figure 10.1

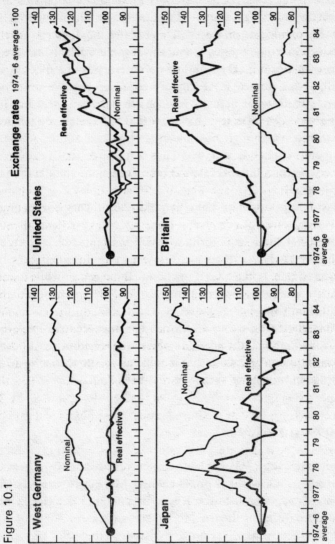

Exchange rates 1974–6 average = 100

United States

West Germany

Britain

Japan

the best guide to competitiveness in different countries is to compare unit wage costs – the total wage bill divided by the number of widgets produced. This isolates the domestic costs of production from other costs (such as raw materials) which are set largely in world markets and so do not vary between countries.

How well does a P.P.P. theory based on relative unit wage costs explain what actually happens in currency markets? If it was always accurate, it would show that real exchange rates were constant even though nominal rates bounced about. As figure 10.1 shows, that is not what has happened; in Britain's and America's case, the real rate has been even more volatile than the nominal rate.

P.P.P. supporters do not claim that their theory covers all the twists and turns of currencies; it merely indicates their long-run tendency towards equilibrium, where the real exchange rate is stable. But note that there are different ways of changing the real exchange rate. It can alter if the nominal rate varies while relative unit wage costs do not; or if the nominal rate is constant while relative unit wage costs move.

This choice raises an issue that has been central to several previous chapters: the speed at which wages and prices adjust to restore equilibrium. Keep that in mind as you go through various short-term models of exchange-rate behaviour.

Moving prices

Whether or not P.P.P. explains why currencies change, it begs the question of what makes prices change. Monetarist-cum-classical economists give one answer, Keynesians another. This leads them to deduce different theories about exchange rates.

To monetarists, prices move in response to earlier changes in the domestic money supply. If monetary growth exceeds the underlying growth rate of real G.D.P., the excess shows up as inflation. This theory is easily extended to exchange rates. Monetarists think that the speed of monetary growth in one economy relative to another will largely determine how the exchange rate between the two currencies moves. Suppose it is in equilibrium in period one, with £1 = $2. In period two, Britain doubles its money supply while America's stays the same. With twice as many pounds around, each one is worth only half as many dollars as before; the new equilibrium exchange rate is £1 = $1.

The monetarist approach assumes 'the law of one price': any goods and services that can be traded internationally will be priced in their home market at the world equilibrium price. If producers of oil try to charge their domestic customers more than the world price, the customers will go to foreign suppliers until the domestic price is forced down. In practice, transport costs do allow for some difference in prices; and trade barriers (including 'non-tariff barriers' like convoluted customs procedures) may stop domestic buyers getting what they want from the world market. When markets are open, however, monetarists think that the law of one price does rule.

Monetarists add two refinements to their model. First, they say that real economic growth affects exchange rates, because it affects the demand for money. If Britain is growing faster than America, some of the extra supply of pounds will be used to finance faster-growing real transactions; so not all of it will go to pushing down the sterling–dollar exchange rate.

Second, monetarists (like other theorists) include expectations as an influence on exchange rates. With the rational-expectations approach, of course, an exchange rate already embodies all available facts about the future – including a view on the 'fundamental' forces driving exchange rates (in monetarist eyes, relative monetary growth and relative output growth).

Keynesians have a different approach. They say that companies set prices by working out their costs and then adding a profit mark-up. Since costs (particularly wages) change slowly, prices may depart from their international norm for long stretches. If some exogenous shock – political uncertainty, the discovery of oil – pushes a country's exchange rate off its P.P.P. equilibrium, it may take years to return. However, Keynesians explain these departures from P.P.P. by their view of currency overshooting (see later).

So far this chapter has hardly mentioned interest rates as an influence on exchange rates. Yet the fund managers who shift cash from one country to another seem to behave as though interest rates matter. So a new theory has developed, called 'portfolio balance'. It starts by looking at how people hold their financial wealth – divided, for simplicity, between money and bonds – and extends this to include foreign money and foreign bonds. As an earlier chapter explained, in a closed economy the interest rate is what determines the demand for money relative to the demand for bonds. When foreign assets are included, the exchange rate must be brought in as the other determinant.

The model of an open economy has to deal with two markets – the domestic market for money and the international market for bonds; and two variables that affect both markets – the interest rate and the exchange rate. Figure 10.2 shows how equilibrium is reached in the money and bond markets. As with the IS–LM curves of earlier chapters, the two curves in figure 10.2 are derived from various identities and judgements about people's behaviour. For simplicity, their full pedigree is not described here; in essence,

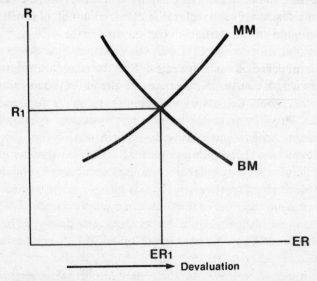

Figure 10.2

though, it comes from assuming that almost every variable is constant in order to get the relationship between interest rates and the exchange rate.

Some of these assumptions will shortly be relaxed. For the moment, see what they mean for the two curves in figure 10.2.

The MM curve deals with the money market; when interest rates rise, people want to hold less money. But the model assumes that the money supply is constant. So the only way that people will be satisfied with their existing money balances is by becoming richer. The only way that can happen is through a devaluation of the exchange rate, which increases the domestic-currency value of their holdings of foreign bonds. Taking the money market by itself, a rise in interest rates therefore needs a devaluation to restore equilibrium – giving an upward-sloping MM curve.

The BM curve deals with the bond market; it represents all the combinations of interest rates and exchange rates at which the bond market is in equilibrium. It slopes down from left to right because higher interest rates in country X will mean that residents want to hold more of their portfolio in domestic bonds. Since the supply of those bonds is fixed, the only way they will be satisfied with their existing portfolio is if the domestic-currency value of their foreign bonds falls. This can happen if the exchange rate rises.

This model comes alive when you relax the assumptions about what is held constant. Suppose, for example, that the supply of domestic bonds increases because the government runs a budget deficit. The BM curve will shift to the right – to BM_2, in figure 10.3 – because the residents of country X will need higher interest rates to persuade them to hold more bonds. But wealth effects mean that they feel richer, so want to hold more money – shifting the MM curve out to MM_2.

The combined effect of these shifts certainly raises the interest rate, to R_2. However, its effect on the exchange rate is ambiguous. The way that figure 10.3 has been drawn produces a devaluation of the exchange rate, from ER_1 to ER_2; but if the MM curve shifted more, it would result in the exchange rate appreciating, even at the higher level of interest rates.

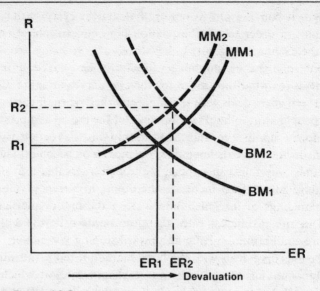

Figure 10.3

Ambiguity also emerges when the foreign interest rate rises. It will shift both curves to the right – which would clearly devalue the exchange rate of currency X. But its effect on interest rates in country X will depend on how much each curve shifts.

The only unequivocal effects come from: (1) an increase in country X's money supply. This devalues its exchange rate and reduces its interest rate. (2) A rise in the foreign-currency value of the foreign assets held by residents of country X – the result, for example, of country X running an external current-account surplus which therefore enables it to buy more foreign assets. This will cause X's exchange rate to appreciate, but its interest rate will not be changed. You can confirm both these effects by drawing your own versions of figure 10.2 and shifting the curves about.

The three basic theories of exchange rates – Keynesian, monetarist and portfolio-balance – can help to answer a specific question about the fourth, P.P.P. Even supposing that exchange rates tend towards a P.P.P. equilibrium, in the real world they 'overshoot' in the short term – they rise or fall more than is needed to restore P.P.P.

Why? One explanation is that domestic prices and wages adjust only sluggishly to a change in nominal exchange rates. In a two-country world, suppose that the exchange rate is in P.P.P. equilibrium; then country A doubles its money supply. In time, that will double its prices and wages, so its exchange rate will need to halve to restore P.P.P. If prices and wages doubled immediately, the currency markets would also immediately halve the exchange rate. Immediately afterwards, price stability would return, so nominal interest rates would not have to change; equilibrium would immediately be re-established. But if prices and wages take time to rise, then the doubling of the nominal money supply will increase the real money supply as well. In that case, interest rates will fall. Money will leave the country through its capital account.

To prevent that happening, the exchange rate has to fall immediately — not just to its eventual P.P.P. equilibrium, but below it. This overshooting is needed to persuade people that the next move in the exchange rate will be up. When they know that, they will be happy to go on holding the currency. Their expected capital gain compensates them for earning less interest than they could in other currencies, even though interest rates have fallen. In time, wages and prices will catch up with the doubling of the money supply. As they do, the real value of the money supply falls; interest rates rise; and the exchange rate gradually rises back to its new P.P.P. equilibrium, where it will be worth half its initial value.

Note one big implication of this analysis for the real economy. It says that a change in the nominal exchange rate has no lasting effect on an economy's competitiveness; a currency devaluation will eventually produce higher domestic wages and prices, cancelling out any benefit it may initially have brought.

This sounds familiar. It is the international version of the conclusion reached in earlier chapters that dealt with a closed economy: the supply curve is vertical, so output cannot be permanently expanded by a fiscal or monetary expansion of demand. What divides economists, internationally as domestically, is how quickly wages and prices move.

11 How payments balance

A country's links with the rest of the world can have a big influence on its economy. As world trade grows and capital moves more freely between countries, so economic theorists have paid more attention to what determines the balance of payments.

Economists are often accused of obfuscation, yet much of their theory is deliberately over-simplified. They often find it convenient to analyse a 'closed' economy – one with no trading or financial links with other countries. When this assumption is relaxed, economic models become more cluttered. But their essence does not change in unexpected ways. For example, classical-cum-monetarist economists base their view of the balance of payments on the same broad principles of market flexibility that they use in closed-economy models.

Before considering the different balance-of-payments theories, start with some simple arithmetic and basic economics. Arithmetically, a country's balance of payments has two main parts.

The current account

This covers imports and exports of goods and services; the interest, profits and dividends received from abroad and paid to foreigners; remittances – the cash that foreign workers send home; and some minor public-sector transfers.

The capital account

Money lent or invested abroad makes up the capital account. It can be short-term – Britons with American bank deposits that can be filled or emptied by a single telephone call; or long-term, as when multinational companies and foreign-aid agencies invest in big projects that may take years to complete.

By definition, the balance of payments must balance. A country with a $1 billion deficit on its current account must get $1 billion in foreign currency to finance it. Often it will do that by running a surplus on its capital account – a matching inflow of $1 billion. But most countries have official reserves of foreign currency and gold that they can use to cover their current-account deficit, at least for a time. So the current account minus the capital account plus any change in official reserves adds up to zero.

This is just the same as any individual's personal finances. He can spend more than he earns (a current-account deficit) provided he can borrow (a capital-account surplus); otherwise he must use his savings (reserves) to bridge the gap.

Now apply some economics to this arithmetic. Whether the official reserves do or do not change depends on a country's exchange-rate policy. Under the Bretton Woods system of fixed rates, central banks frequently intervened in currency markets. If their exchange rate was under pressure to devalue, they sold foreign exchange from their reserves in order to buy (and so support) their own currency. Those countries with upward pressure on their rate, like Japan and West Germany in the late 1960s and early 1970s, bought foreign currency so as to provide foreigners with the yen or D-marks they wanted. This central-bank intervention had a big effect on countries' official reserves. Perhaps the main reason why a currency was eventually forced to devalue was that its government was running out of reserves to support it.

With freely floating exchange rates, none of this need matter. Central banks do not buy or sell currencies. A current-account surplus (or deficit) is entirely matched by a deficit (surplus) on the capital account. Foreign reserves do not change. In practice floating has seldom been entirely clean since the Bretton Woods system collapsed in 1973, so countries have used their reserves occasionally.

The exchange-rate policy chosen by a government has implications for the domestic economy. At this stage, note one in particular: what happens to the money supply. Suppose Japan has a $5 billion surplus on its balance of payments, with its central bank increasing its foreign reserves rather than letting the yen's exchange rate rise beyond Y250 to the dollar. When Japanese exporters and financial institutions receive the $5 billion, the central bank provides them with the fixed-rate equivalent in yen – Y1.25 trillion. It is therefore boosting the domestic money supply by the amount of the balance-of-payments surplus. To offset this effect on the money supply, it would need to 'sterilize' the surplus by selling more bonds and taking the Y1.25 trillion out of circulation again.

Full equilibrium

When economists study a closed economy, they want to see how its markets for goods and money achieve equilibrium. When they open it up to international trade and financial flows, they want to see how its payments are balanced. These are preliminaries to the bigger question: how does an economy simultaneously reach both internal and external equilibrium?

The answer can be best described in terms of the IS–LM model, using the two familiar curves and adding a third.

The IS curve shows the combinations of interest rates and income that produce equilibrium in the goods market. In an open economy it will shift to the right if net exports increase, because aggregate demand will be higher for any particular level of interest rates. Net exports can increase for several reasons, such as a falling exchange rate or growth in foreign markets.

The LM curve shows the money market in equilibrium at different combinations of interest rates and income. For the moment, assume that it does not shift in response to external developments, because the money supply is assumed to be exogenous – because, for example, it is unaffected by a change in the reserves as the central bank is sterilizing.

The BP curve represents the combinations of interest rates and output at which the balance of payments is in equilibrium. Start with a world of fixed exchange rates, and the BP curve sloping up from left to right (see figure 11.1). This indicates that a rise in domestic income worsens the current account, because a country's demand for imports increases more than foreign demand for its exports. As a result, the country has to attract more capital from abroad so as to balance its payments; this requires higher interest rates (though these may have only a one-off effect of luring more capital).

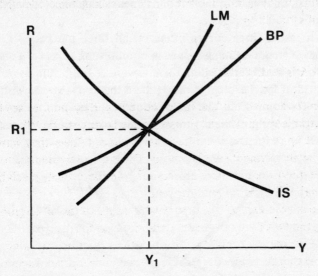

Figure 11.1

What will shift the BP curve? Like the IS curve, it will move to the right if anything happens to increase net exports: faster growth abroad, an exchange-rate devaluation, an improvement in competitiveness because foreign prices rise. The capital-account elements in the BP curve can also make it shift. It will go to the right if, for example, foreign interest rates fall, as the country can then enjoy a more favourable combination of interest rates and output while still balancing its payments.

As the BP curve represents balance-of-payments equilibrium,

what do the areas either side of it signify? Anywhere to the right
of BP in figure 11.1 means that the overall balance of payments is
in deficit – i.e. that a country is drawing on its foreign reserves.
This deficit can occur for either or both of two reasons: (a)
output demanded (Y) is too high, so the country is importing
more than it is exporting – a current-account deficit; and/or (b)
interest rates are too low relative to world rates, so the country
is unable to attract foreign capital and may indeed have
domestic capital flowing abroad – a capital-account deficit. By
contrast, anywhere to the left of BP means a balance-of-payments
surplus.

Where the three curves intersect, all three markets – goods,
money, foreign exchange – are in equilibrium, at R_1Y_1. To show
the forces that keep pushing them towards equilibrium, start with
a world of fixed exchange rates where the BP curve has shifted –
to BP_2 in figure 11.2. The intersection of the IS and LM curves, at
A, is to the right of the BP curve, so the balance of payments is in
deficit.

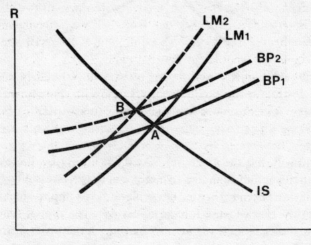

Figure 11.2

By definition, that is not an equilibrium, and it sets off a reaction elsewhere in the economy. The balance-of-payments deficit reduces the money supply, which means that the LM curve shifts to the left. It will keep moving until it reaches LM_2, establishing a new equilibrium at B. Demand is lower and interest rates higher than at A: that is how the economy corrects a balance-of-payments deficit.

Or is it? The conclusion from figure 11.2 depends critically on the slope of the BP curve. Remember that the balance of payments is composed of two parts, current and capital. Other things being equal, a rise in income will 'worsen' the current acount – i.e. give it a smaller surplus or a bigger deficit – because extra domestic spending will suck in more imports. So a BP curve sloping up from left to right shows that a deteriorating current account can be partially offset by an improving capital account, because higher interest rates will attract more capital from abroad.

This case needs to be contrasted with a world – still with fixed exchange rates – where capital (a) does not move at all between countries and (b) moves with complete freedom. In (a), the BP curve is vertical. Any adjustment to the balance of payments has to come through the current account alone – the assumption of most economic theorists in the 1940s and 1950s.

Figure 11.3 shows how the economy will respond in such a world. It starts with an equilibrium, A; suppose that investment then increases for exogenous reasons (e.g. firms expecting higher profits), so the IS curve shifts to IS_2. If the central bank accommodates the increase by keeping interest rates stable at R_1 and supplying more money, the LM curve will shift to LM_2, producing a short-run equilibrium at B. Though that has increased income, it is to the right of the BP curve, so the balance of payments is in deficit. The central bank is holding the exchange rate steady – so it loses reserves, until the government has no option but to cut domestic spending. It will raise taxes or reduce public expenditure or raise interest rates – anything to shift the IS curve back to the left.

Depending on the actual combination of policies, the economy

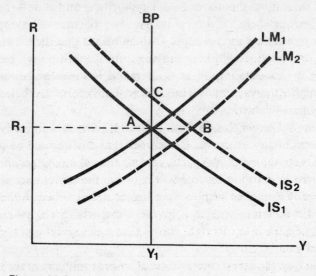

Figure 11.3

will return to equilibrium either at A or at a point above it – but one on the BP curve. The balance of payments is an absolute constraint: income will increase only if the current account improves and shifts the BP curve to the right. When, in the 1960s and early 1970s, British politicians were exhorting companies to export more, this was the model of the economy they were (consciously or not) working from. To them, the balance of payments meant trade in goods: the goods market – the IS curve – was therefore the one that had to adjust.

A monetary approach

Starting in the 1960s, other economic theorists put more stress on monetary factors. Look at the capital account, they said, and at the corresponding changes in the money market – i.e. the LM curve. Even in those days, when capital movements were relatively restricted, it was clear that the capital account often adjusted faster than the current account to disequilibrium in the balance of payments.

The 'monetary approach' to the balance of payments can be applied to any model, no matter what the slope of the BP curve. To see what it means, look again at figure 11.3. When the IS curve shifted to IS$_2$, it was assumed that the central bank would obligingly provide more money to underwrite the shift, so the LM curve would move to LM$_2$. But if the central bank refused to do so, the economy would be at the intersection of IS$_2$ and LM$_1$.

This is to the right of the BP curve, so the balance of payments would be in deficit. This would reduce the reserves – and hence the money supply as well. In that case, the LM curve would shift to the left until it reached C, where IS$_2$ and BP meet. The economy would be back in equilibrium, with the same income but a higher interest rate.

Now take the other extreme case of a horizontal BP curve. This means that capital is perfectly mobile between countries. Investors do not mind which country's bonds they hold, so if the

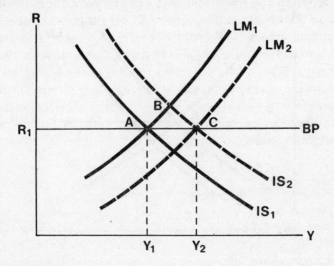

Figure 11.4

interest rate rises in country A they will send money out of country B until rates are again the same. In short, there is a 'world interest rate'.

That rate is set at R_1 in figure 11.4. Again, suppose that the economy starts at full equilibrium at A and that exchange rates are still fixed. If the government tries to raise income with a fiscal boost, it will push the IS curve out to IS_2. At B, the new inter-section with the LM curve, the higher interest rate will attract a rush of capital from abroad. This will boost the money supply, pushing the LM curve down until it reaches LM_2 and interest rates are again back at their world level. The new equilibrium is at C – and income has been increased from Y_1 to Y_2. With fixed exchange rates, a fiscal boost can effectively increase demand.

By contrast, a monetary boost cannot. In figure 11.5, the central bank pushes the LM curve out to LM_2. The IS and LM curves now cross at B – not an equilibrium, because it is off the BP curve. Interest rates are below their world level, so capital leaves the country. It goes on doing so until the money supply

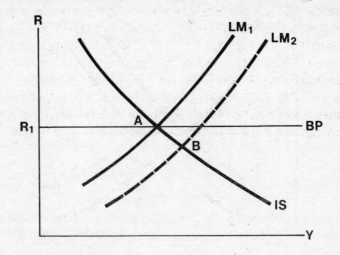

Figure 11.5

has shrunk back to LM_1 and the economy has returned to A: nothing has changed.

The relative effectiveness of fiscal and monetary policy is reversed if exchange rates are floating rather than fixed. There is no balance-of-payments constraint as such – with floating rates, by definition, the current and capital accounts exactly offset each other. So the central bank does not have any international inflow or outflow of capital to try to sterilize; instead the exchange rate itself adjusts.

Suppose that the central bank wants to expand the money supply. The exchange rate will fall; as the previous chapter showed, it will overshoot its eventual equilibrium. In due course, prices will rise by the same proportion as the monetary expansion. Until they have done so, however, the real money supply does increase, so LM_1 can shift out to LM_2 and income rises. This example illustrates an important general rule: governments can choose an exchange-rate target or a money-supply target, but they cannot hit both simultaneously.

Floating exchange rates make it much harder for fiscal policy to increase demand. A fiscal boost will raise interest rates, just as it would in a closed economy, so some private investment and consumption will be 'crowded out' and income will not rise by as much as the fiscal expansion initially suggested. With higher interest rates, the exchange rate would float up. This would expand imports and divert exports; the net trade balance would therefore shrink, further reducing the rise in income.

What about jobs?

This chapter has discussed equilibrium in three markets, all of them on the demand side of the economy. Even when all are in equilibrium, nothing in this model says whether the economy will also be at full employment. As earlier chapters showed, that question can be answered only by including the supply side as well.

Imagine an economy with full employment, but a balance of payments deficit. The IS−LM−BP approach shows that the deficit will be eliminated and equilibrium restored only by cutting demand. But that would also cut employment.

There is a way out of this bind. The balance of payments could be restored by improving the competitiveness of the economy, so that net exports rose without any overall reduction in demand. Improved competitiveness means a fall in the real exchange rate. As the previous chapter made clear, that could be achieved either by devaluing the nominal exchange rate while domestic costs (overwhelmingly, wages) stayed the same; or by reducing costs in nominal terms while the exchange rate was constant.

This highlights the familiar issue of real wages. Just as employment in a closed economy depends on the level of real wages, so it does in an open economy. The critical issues are once again the slope of the supply curve and how quickly wages react to changes in the labour market.

12 Understanding growth

Previous chapters discussed economies that are close to points of short-term equilibrium. This chapter extends the time-scale, and asks how far theory can explain some observed facts of long-term economic growth. Readers beware: growth theory is difficult, and so is this chapter.

Growth theory has lately been out of fashion. It flowered for twenty-five years after the Second World War, developing more rapidly perhaps than any other branch of economics. During that period it often seemed the most important branch too. After all, the post-war Keynesian consensus had abolished unemployment; economics was free to move on from the short-term problems of stabilization policy to the weightier issue of long-term growth. In the 1970s and 1980s, however, the day-to-day problems of economic management were thrust back to the top of the agenda.

More importantly, the theories of the 1950s and 1960s seemed to run into a dead end. With great ingenuity and mathematical sophistication, researchers came up with models roughly consistent with the broad facts of growth, but there were no clear conclusions for policy. If anything, the thrust of the research was that governments could do little to influence the long-run rate of growth – in either direction. That seemed implausible, and it was certainly not what policymakers wanted to hear. Moreover, the models themselves were not empirically robust; they prompted the most intractable problems of data and measurement that economics has so far encountered, so much of the research has been impossible to test or apply.

The starting point for any theory of growth is the idea of equilibrium – a long-run counterpart to the static equilibrium that underpins the theories discussed in earlier chapters. This evolving sort of equilibrium is called a 'steady state'. Growth theories try to describe a special kind of steady state: one where the economy stays at full employment, with a fixed ratio of capital to labour, while output grows at a constant rate. Economists want the theory to say whether an economy can find its own way to such a steady state, and to show what happens inside the economy as it travels along the steady-state path.

Because growth theories take full employment for granted, they are concerned with potential, rather than actual, output; the difference between the two is a matter for short-term stabilization policy. Is a theory of growth in potential output any use? Yes, provided policy can change in a steady-state fashion to accommodate that growth and hold the economy at full employment. The short-term model discussed in earlier chapters – the IS–LM model of demand, and the labour-market model of supply – shows that policy can adjust in the required way.

To see this, suppose that the growth of potential output is simply the sum of two other growth rates: the growth of the labour force, and the growth of labour productivity, or real output per worker. So if the labour force is growing at 2 per cent a year and output per worker at 3 per cent a year, the potential growth in output is 5 per cent a year. Graphically, the aggregate-supply curve shifts continuously to the right, as in the top half of figure 12.1.

What happens to prices as potential output grows? If the split of national income between wages and profits does not change over time, then it follows mathematically that the long-run inflation rate must equal the growth of wages less the growth of output per worker. Suppose that wage increases of 5 per cent a year are consistent with 'full employment' (this is a Phillips-curve relationship, as discussed in chapter 8); with output per worker rising at 3 per cent a year, the trend inflation rate will therefore be 2 per cent a year.

As a result, the price level rises in figure 12.1 along with output. The problem for monetary and fiscal policy is to move the aggregate-demand curve so that it cuts the shifting supply

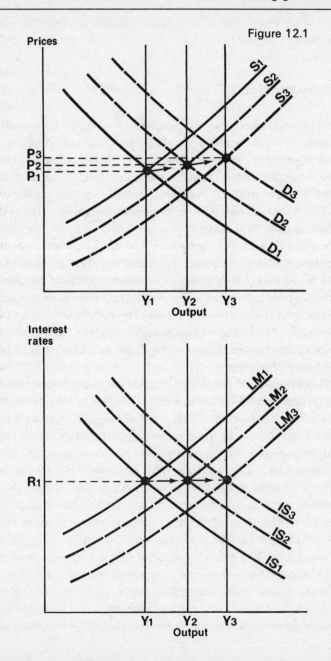

Figure 12.1

curve at an ever-rising price level – equivalent to price inflation of 2 per cent a year.

Policy choices

If interest rates were rising or falling, the growth path could not be a steady state. Monetary policy must therefore shift the LM curve in the lower part of figure 12.1 so that the money market stays in equilibrium without a change in interest rates as output grows. The required rate of increase in the money supply depends on the exact form of the demand-for-money relationship embodied in the LM curve.

Suppose that the demand for money doubles when aggregate demand doubles; in that case, the money supply must grow at the same rate as aggregate demand to move LM along the desired track. Aggregate demand is simply the real growth in output (5 per cent a year in our example) plus the change in prices (2 per cent a year). Hence the monetary authorities need to increase the money supply by 7 per cent a year to hold the economy in balance as it grows along trend.

What about fiscal policy? Remember the IS curve embodies an equilibrium condition for the goods market, and one way to think of that condition is that total planned savings and total planned investment in the economy must be equal. In the long term the private sector saves a more-or-less constant fraction of its income; likewise, the proportion of income invested in new physical capacity should not change much. As income grows, therefore, savings and investment will both grow at the same rate, automatically shifting the IS curve to the right, as in figure 12.1, and maintaining demand-side equilibrium.

One caveat. There is no guarantee that the savings ratio and the investment ratio, though constant, will be equal to each other at this particular level of interest rates (R_1 in figure 12.1). If they are different, demand-side balance requires a government deficit (if savings exceed investment) or surplus (if vice versa) to square the accounts. And as the economy grows, the money value of that deficit (or surplus) must grow too – just enough to maintain a constant ratio of deficit (or surplus) to total output.

All this means that the model described in earlier chapters can preserve full employment as potential output grows along a steady-state path. On our illustrative assumptions, for example, the economy could stay at full employment if: output grows at 5 per cent a year (3 per cent of which is due to rising output per worker); inflation runs at 2 per cent a year; wages rise by 5 per cent a year; and the money supply expands by 7 per cent a year.

To complete the picture, suppose that a fiscal deficit of 2 per cent of output were needed each year to equate savings and investment and balance the goods market. So as not to interfere with the path of monetary growth, any deficit must be financed by selling government bonds. The arithmetic of debt finance then tells us that the ratio of government debt to output would eventually settle down to a constant 40 per cent – 2/5, the fiscal deficit divided by the growth rate of output.

Finding the path

A trickier question is whether potential output will ever find its way onto a steady-state growth path. The forerunner of modern growth theories – the Harrod-Domar model – concluded that it almost certainly would not. This model assumed that (a) the labour force grows at a constant rate, n per cent a year; (b) savings and investment are equal to each other, and to a fixed fraction of output, s per cent; and (c) extra output always needs fixed proportions of labour and capital – in other words, doubling output would need exactly twice as much labour and twice as much capital.

The important assumption is (c); it is equivalent to saying that firms cannot substitute labour for capital, or vice versa. Every extra unit of output requires a fixed amount of extra capital – traditionally this number is called v. With this assumption, the

Harrod-Domar model says that steady-state growth will only happen if s, the savings rate, divided by v, the ratio of capital to output, is equal to n, the rate of growth of the labour force.

This is not as hard as it looks. Remember s is really savings divided by output, and v is capital divided by output; so s divided by v is savings divided by capital – output cancels out. But savings divided by capital is just the rate of growth of the capital stock. The Harrod-Domar condition for steady growth simply says that capital and the labour force must expand at the same rate.

Suppose that the labour force grew faster. The excess labour could not be taken into productive work because of assumption (c); unemployment would rise indefinitely, so there could be no steady state. If, on the other hand, the capital stock grew faster than the labour force, excess plant capacity would accumulate for exactly the same reason. Again, no steady state.

Note that the model assumes that s, v, and n are fixed independently. There is no *a priori* reason to think that they will satisfy the Harrod-Domar condition; but if they do not, the model predicts that the economy will never reach this knife-edge equilibrium; it will be perpetually unstable, with an ever-widening gap between potential and actual output. Real-world economies do not behave like that. Evidently, the Harrod-Domar assumptions are wrong, and one or more of the three variables, s, v, and n must vary in a way that prevents a continuous build-up of excess men or machines.

The most plausible candidate is v, the capital–output ratio. Allowing it to vary as the economy adjusts to the steady state is equivalent to saying that labour and capital, at least to some extent, can be used as substitutes for each other. That seems reasonable. Professor Robert Solow of the Massachusetts Institute of Technology devised a model incorporating this assumption, and prompted a batch of similar theories that were jointly christened 'neoclassical' (yet another use for that over-worked word).

Figure 12.2 shows how these neoclassical models work. It plots

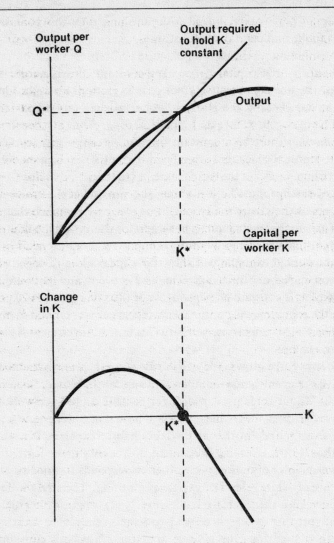

Figure 12.2

output per worker against capital per worker. The curved line in the top half of figure 12.2 is a production function (familiar from chapter 3), which says that output per worker rises with additions to capital per worker, but at a diminishing rate; this confirms that labour and capital are substitutes.

The other line in the top half of figure 12.2 represents the output required to hold capital per worker constant; this is harder to grasp. The line contains two kinds of information. First, the idea that savings – as in the Harrod-Domar model – are a constant fraction of output. (Since the labour force is growing at a constant rate, savings must be a constant fraction of output per worker, too.) Second, the idea that capital per worker will be constant once the economy reaches the steady state. At that point, therefore, the flow of savings must be just enough to provide capital for new workers as they enter the labour force – but not so much that it gives existing workers more. The jargon for this is that the flow of savings must widen capital in the economy without deepening it.

A numerical example will show how these ideas fit together. Suppose the labour force is growing at 2 per cent, and that output per worker is constant at 100 widgets. If the savings rate is 20 per cent, the economy will consume 80 widgets per worker and save – i.e. invest – 20 widgets per worker. This flow of investment is just enough to hold capital per worker constant at 1,000 widgets as the labour force grows. Why 1,000? Because then the investment flow is 2 per cent of the initial level of capital per worker, matching the labour-force growth of 2 per cent. If capital per worker were more than 1,000 widgets, a flow of only 20 widgets would reduce capital per worker as the labour force expands. If it was less than 1,000, the same investment flow would make it rise.

So each level of output per worker corresponds to some stable – i.e. steady-state – level of capital per worker. The straight line in figure 12.2 shows this relationship. It is straight rather than curved because its slope depends on the savings rate and the growth rate of the labour force, and these are both constant. Where it cuts the production function, output per worker (Q^*) and capital per worker (K^*) are at their steady-state levels: actual output per worker equals the output required to generate the savings that will hold capital per worker constant.

Is this steady-state a knife-edge too? No, as is confirmed by the

lower half of figure 12.2. Suppose output per worker is less than
Q*. Output is higher than the required level – the economy is
investing so much that the capital stock is growing faster than the
labour force, and capital per worker is therefore rising. The extra
capital per worker pushes output per worker along the production
function; output per worker stops rising only at Q*K*. The same
argument works in reverse if output starts at a level higher than
Q*. The equilibrium at Q*K* is stable: if knocked away from it,
the economy will return.

Moving the path

Output per worker is assumed to be constant in this steady state.
The model therefore says that the economy is always moving
towards a long-term equilibrium in which total output grows at
the same rate as the labour force. However, two refinements to
the model allow for faster growth than that.

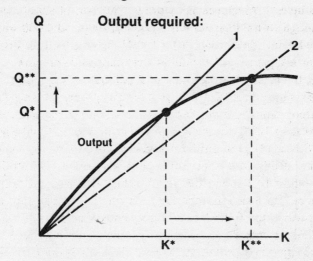

Figure 12.3

Changing the savings rate

Starting from Q*K* in figure 12.3, a rise in the savings rate would flatten the output-required line – the extra savings can finance a higher level of capital per worker as the labour force grows. The rise in capital per worker increases output per worker to a new equilibrium, at Q**K**. When the economy reaches that point it grows again at the same pace as the labour force, but in the interim the shift in output per worker pushes the growth rate higher. Between steady states, in other words, the economy can grow faster than its long-term rate if the government stimulates savings – through tax reform, perhaps.

Figure 12.4 compares this kind of growth with the three others already discussed, by tracing output through time. The first kind of growth happens when an economy moves from a point of unemployment to full employment – the burst of growth caused by expansionary fiscal and/or monetary policy. This is the shift from A to B in figure 12.4. Then there is the growth that happens as the economy approaches its steady state. In figure 12.2, for example, this happens as output per worker rises to Q*; in figure 12.4 it is the shift from B to C. Third, there is growth along the steady-state path itself, at the same rate as growth in the labour

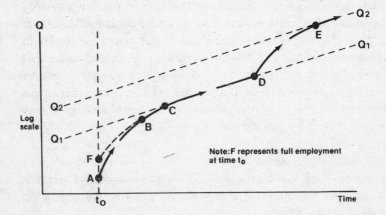

Figure 12.4

force – from C to D. Finally, from D to E, we have the growth that happens when an economy shifts from one steady state to another.

Changing the savings ratio thus alters the level of the steady-state path, but not its slope. This raises an interesting question which a separate strand of the growth literature has tried to answer: if the government can fix the savings rate, and shift the economy's long-run growth path, what rate should it pick?

The mathematics of optimal growth can be fearsomely complicated, but a partial answer to the problem is the so-called 'golden rule of accumulation'. The idea is to find the savings rate that maximizes consumption over all future years. As the savings rate rises, so does the ratio of capital to labour, and with it the level of the output path. But at the same time, the proportion of each successive gain in output that has to be put back into investment is rising too. The reason for this is that the path we are looking for is itself a steady state, which means that it has a constant ratio of capital per worker. With a growing labour force, a bigger capital stock imposes an ever-bigger burden of future investment to hold that ratio steady.

As the production function flattens out (see figures 12.2 and 12.3), higher savings will eventually reach a point where they increase future output by less than they raise the required amount of future investment – in other words, they cause a lower path of future consumption. Crunching through the maths shows that optimal growth requires enough savings to raise capital per worker to the point where the rate of return on capital just equals the rate of growth of the labour force. Improbable as it may sound, that is the golden rule of growth!

Technical progress

The simple models discussed so far all focus on capital accumulation – i.e. the quantity of capital. What about changes in the quality of inputs?

The easiest way to take technical progress into account is to assume that labour productivity (with a given capital stock) rises at a constant rate. This is equivalent to an increase in labour input; so it affects the steady-state conditions in exactly the same way as faster growth in the labour supply does. For example, the slope of the steady-state growth path between c and d in figure 12.4 becomes the growth in the labour force plus the increase in labour productivity.

This kind of progress – economists call it 'labour-augmenting disembodied technical progress' – does alter the long-term growth rate. It also helps the neoclassical growth model to fit the so-called 'stylized facts' of growth. These broad empirical observations seem to hold for most industrial countries; the most important are (a) the growth of output and the labour force is fairly steady, but output growth is faster than labour-force growth; (b) the capital stock grows at a steady rate, roughly as fast as output; therefore (c) the capital–output ratio is constant.

Unfortunately, disembodied technical progress is really a theoretical cop-out. 'Disembodied' means that growth is not linked to improvements – due to better training, for example – in particular generations of workers; it showers down like manna from heaven, affecting old lags and new boys alike. It is as if every journalist in Britain woke up one day and knew how to touch-type. A shift of this kind may sometimes happen once and for all – for example, a Thatcher effect on trade union restrictive practices, perhaps. But it is unlikely to take place continuously.

Productivity in the real world is more likely to rise because of 'capital-embodied' technical progress – new machines are more efficient than old, so the productivity of the capital stock gradually rises as new vintages come on stream. But according to present theories this kind of progress is like an increase in the savings rate; it can increase the steady-state rate of growth only temporarily.

Suppose that, thanks to new investment, the average age of the capital stock is falling; if new machines are more efficient, there will be an extra amount of output growth every year as the stock gets younger. However, the average age of the capital stock cannot fall indefinitely; eventually it must reach an equilibrium average age, and at that point the economy will resume its previous steady-state path. The only consolation is that it might take many years to reduce the average age of the capital stock to its equilibrium point; in the meantime, the economy can enjoy faster-than-steady-state growth.

These models all leave much to be desired. They seem to fit the facts of growth only when one of the central issues for policy – the diffusion of technical change – is swept under the carpet of 'disembodied progress'. New research will advance by exploring models with more than one sector – i.e. economies that produce separate goods for investment and consumption, rather than the all-purpose widgets of this chapter that can be eaten, worn, lived in, driven around town – and used to make other widgets. But the underlying problem of measuring changes in the quality of capital will remain. There may be no limits to growth, but perhaps economics is near the limits of growth theory.

13 The economics of poverty

The previous chapter discussed growth without making any distinction between rich and poor countries. This chapter looks at the recent controversy over whether economics needs a separate branch of theory to understand the problems of underdevelopment.

Until the mid-1960s very few economists questioned the legitimacy of development economics. It seemed obvious that the 'less-developed countries' (L.D.C.s) had their own special problems; widespread poverty was considered a sign that conventional economics was irrelevant. A separate literature had flourished, treating the L.D.C.s as a class apart. Then, from the mid-1960s, disillusionment set in. Within a few years a neoclassical revival that mirrored many of the changes going on in mainstream economics came up with new ideas (which were often old ideas) on the causes and cures of economic backwardness. All this happened in a way that undermined the very idea of 'development economics'.

All the signs suggest that development economics is now in decline as a theoretical discipline. The number of new theoretical studies published has fallen sharply; the subject is out of vogue among graduate students launching their careers as academics; universities struggle to fill their development professorships when they fall vacant. The clearest sign of all: the controversy over the field's right to exist is now its most vibrant debate – witness 'Pioneers in Development', a set of new essays by the subject's best brains, published by the World Bank. In some ways it is surprising that this counter-revolution has gone so far: the post-war development efforts can claim their successes, and many of the theoretical issues at stake are far from settled.

The early approach to development theory started with a puzzle: why is it harder for countries that are poor in the second half of the twentieth century to grow than it was for Britain and the rest of Europe in the nineteenth century? Today's poor countries of the south can draw on a hundred years of northern technical progress in modernizing their economies; they do not have to make those breakthroughs themselves. Theory answered the puzzle by saying that it can be hard to apply a technology even if it is already available; L.D.C.s find it especially hard to follow the path of the early industrializers for four mutually-reinforcing reasons.

Rural underemployment

The most influential model in traditional development economics was set out by Sir Arthur Lewis in 1954, in a paper called 'Economic Development with Unlimited Supplies of Labour'. It assumed that L.D.C.s are divided into a backward agricultural sector – with so much surplus labour that a fall in the labour force would leave output unchanged – and a smaller industrial sector. Growth requires a bigger industrial sector, and hence a flow of workers from farms to factories. The trouble is that importing the capital equipment needed by industry is not enough to ensure economic growth; if agricultural productivity fails to keep pace, development will stop.

Figure 13.1 shows why. D_1 represents the demand for industrial workers – it is a demand-for-labour curve just like those of earlier chapters. The going wage-rate, w_1, is higher than the average income of agricultural workers; at that wage, L_1 workers are employed in industry. The model expects profits – initially shown by the area $w_1 A' F_2$, – to be reinvested, and as the capital stock expands, the demand for industrial labour shifts outwards, to D_2.

At the same time, however, the demand for agricultural output is likely to rise, partly because the labour force as a whole now has a higher total income, and partly because most L.D.C.s have a growing population. Unless farm output can increase, higher demand will force up food prices relative to industrial prices,

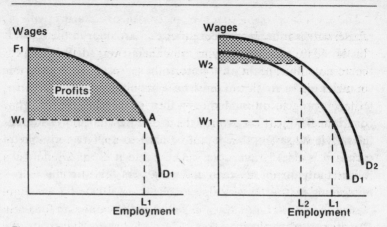

Figure 13.1

which in turn means that the factories must pay their workers more to attract them into industry. As a result, profits fall, and so does investment in the emerging industrial economy. Low productivity on the farms, by prompting a rise in agricultural prices, therefore chokes development.

Lack of resources for investment

A country generates the money it needs for investment through savings – in other words, by producing more than it consumes. L.D.C.s face two special difficulties in doing that. Because they are so poor, it is particularly hard for them to sacrifice current consumption for future increases in welfare; personal incomes may be at or below subsistence levels to begin with. In addition, L.D.C.s need to buy capital goods that will almost always have to be imported; so development also hinges on ready supplies of foreign exchange.

These resource shortages gave rise to numerous 'two-gap' models of poor-country growth – the savings gap is the inability of the L.D.C.s to hold down consumption in order to finance a high rate of investment, and the trade gap is their inability to finance imports of needed capital goods through export earnings. The question was, how to fill those gaps?

Adverse trends in world prices

In the 1950s and 1960s many economists argued that L.D.C.s could not afford to follow a historically typical growth path, one in which different sectors, including farming, advance together, balancing each other and avoiding economic strains. They quarrelled in particular with the idea that the poor countries should develop their agriculture and then exchange exports of primary goods for imported manufactures. That would be a mistake, they argued, because of long-term price trends.

According to a theory developed in the 1950s by Mr Raúl Prebisch, of the United Nations Economic Commission for Latin America, and Professor Hans Singer of Sussex University, the price of primary goods is bound to fall over time relative to the price of manufactures. This will cause a long-term deterioration in the L.D.C.s' terms of trade (the ratio of their export prices to their import prices) – unless the poor countries make it their top priority to develop their industry.

Table 13.1

Ratio of primary commodity prices to manufactured export prices
(1957 = 100)

	Foods	Beverages	Agricultural raw materials	Metals
1957	100	100	100	100
1960	92	78	97	92
1965	91	67	61	114
1970	91	75	63	111
1975	111	58	61	76
1980	96	82	67	82
1982	73	73	55	72

Source: IMF

The Prebisch–Singer thesis seems easy to test, and the figures in table 13.1 apparently bear it out: they show that the real price of primary goods (except oil) has fallen in the past two decades. Unfortunately, however, these figures cannot settle the matter because they are based on unit value indices (U.V.I.s) rather than true price indices. Statisticians calculate U.V.I.s by dividing quantities of goods into total value; in turn they estimate the quantity of manufactures by weight. As technical progress makes manufactures lighter, U.V.I.s come to be based on an under-estimate of their quantity and thus they overestimate the corresponding 'price'. (This is a good example of how simple questions can drag on in development economics, unresolved for lack of reliable data.)

Bottlenecks and rigidities

The traditional development theorists emphasized that L.D.C.s have a very primitive economic infrastructure. By this they meant more than lack of roads, communications, and financial and other services. Their point was that markets in L.D.C.s cannot be relied upon to correct shortages and redirect resources as they do in more advanced economies.

This frustrates development in many ways; economists cited 'structural inflation', and misguided attempts to deal with it, as one of the most important. According to this theory, inflation in L.D.C.s (and especially in Latin America) was not caused by excess demand, but by bottlenecks that the economy encounters as it grows: shortages of materials, skilled labour and foreign exchange, for example. These bottlenecks meant that inflation was inevitable if the economy was to advance at all; governments could stop it only with deflationary policies so severe that they would stop growth too.

Few members of the post-war development school were willing to accept every aspect of this diagnosis, but these four elements formed a broad consensus. They had a common theme: the necessary market mechanisms for economic growth either did not exist or could not be relied upon to function properly. More importantly, a set of policy prescriptions seemed to follow naturally.

First and foremost, the call was for planning. If governments intervened, the argument went, they could help to overcome all four kinds of obstacle to development. They could ease the rural underemployment constraint by steering the economy on a path of 'balanced growth' (a catch-phrase of the time), in which some resources were put into improving agricultural productivity, as part of the main race to industrialization. They could also fill the two investment gaps of domestic savings and foreign exchange – one by raising taxes and printing money to pay for state-directed capital formation (i.e. forced saving), the other by promoting the growth of firms that made substitutes for imports (which would save precious foreign currency). Foreign aid, unambiguously a good thing according to this view, would also help to fill the gaps; but governments would have to plan how to spend the money.

At the same time, a strategy of industrialization based on import substitution would save the L.D.C.s from the cruel logic of the Prebisch–Singer thesis – first, by reducing their dependence on foreign manufactures, and second, by increasing the ratio of industrial to agricultural goods in their exports. Finally, there seemed an obvious role for planning in directing resources towards the L.D.C.s' supply bottlenecks, and in making the resource-allocation decisions that free markets would handle if only they worked properly.

What went wrong?

The post-war consensus did not come under fire because its prescriptions led the L.D.C.s into economic stagnation. Far from it. Between 1960 and 1973 the poor countries managed an average real G.N.P. growth rate of 6.1 per cent a year; the industrial countries' average over the same period was 4.9 per cent. Even though the L.D.C.s had rapidly rising populations, growth at that rate allowed them to raise real G.N.P. per head by 3.6 per cent a year. This was better than they had ever achieved before.

Economists then began to ask whether the L.D.C.s should not be doing better still – and whether the traditional policies were a help or a hindrance. Adding urgency to this scepticism was the fact that political failures – as the rich countries saw them –

tainted the L.D.C.s' limited economic success. Some politicians and economists on the 'right wing' in rich countries wondered, for example, whether foreign aid was such a good thing. To them, it seemed to promote a dangerous trend towards governments that were centralized, authoritarian, and – all too often – corrupt. Other critics, arguing from the 'left', thought that northern-inspired 'development' was widening income inequalities in the poor countries, and in some cases making the very poorest worse off in absolute terms. Still others said that these policies were perpetuating colonial relationships, and consolidating the poor countries' helpless dependence on their rich patrons. Such worries bred an unlikely alliance of critics from across the political spectrum: neo-conservatives, neo-Marxists and all points between.

The most influential attack on the traditional approach, however, struck at its economic foundations. The case for planning and for other forms of government intervention rested on a belief that markets in L.D.C.s – if they existed at all – did not work. Three of the four obstacles to growth discussed above can be seen in these terms: the problem of disguised unemployment is a kind of breakdown in the labour market; the two-gap diagnosis says that the market for investible funds is not doing its job; supply bottlenecks and rigidities speak of a failure of incentives to move workers and other economic resources to where they are needed.

Empirical evidence began to mount that this story of market failure was heavily exaggerated. In came numerous studies to show that markets do work in the poor countries; that price signals do shift effort and materials, even among illiterate peasants; that the entrepreneurial spirit is there to be nudged. This evidence was accompanied by the already-familiar stories of aid fiascos: millions of dollars in scarce capital wasted on prestige projects of little economic worth, mega-schemes bungled through bureaucratic incompetence. It was no longer obvious that governments in L.D.C.s could do a better job than markets.

The policy of import substitution was perhaps the most

damaging failure. It almost always meant protecting the new industries with tariffs and quotas. With quantitive controls on trade, governments could then ignore the exchange rate – and ignoring it meant letting it get overvalued. That was a large and growing discouragement to exports. And an overvalued exchange rate made everything foreign seem cheap – including foreign bank loans. It is no coincidence that today's biggest L.D.C. debtors – Brazil, Mexico and Argentina – were also the strongest proponents of import substitution in the 1960s and 1970s. By contrast, the development successes were all countries that favoured export promotion – Singapore, Hong Kong, Taiwan and South Korea.

Generalizing no more

This wide range of development experiences was itself a blow to the conventional way of thinking – an L.D.C. was an L.D.C., and that was that. As table 13.2 shows, some L.D.C.s have grown quickly, some slowly; some, like Zaïre, have seen real incomes per head actually fall. Some are desperately poor, others not so poor. Some are over-populated, others under-populated. Some are rich in natural resources, others have little but labour. Some are politically stable, others ready to explode. In short, the differences between L.D.C.s are often greater than the differences between the least poor among them and the rich countries of the north: Brazil is more like Spain than like Chad. Yet the idea that L.D.C.s were a group apart was the core of the traditional approach.

The empirical observation that L.D.C.s were heterogeneous coincided, in the 1970s, with a theoretical climate that suited it perfectly. Mainstream macroeconomic theory was changing in similar ways. Years earlier, the Keynesian revolution had undermined the faith that economics placed in markets – especially the labour market. The post-war consensus on development had similar theoretical leanings, not just through the obvious and eminently Keynesian link of the rural underemployment

Table 13.2

G.N.P., population and life expectancy

	G.N.P. per head $, 1983	Annual average real growth 1965–83	Population (m) mid-1983	Life expectancy, years, 1983
China	300	4.4	1,019.0	67
India	260	1.5	733.2	55
Zaïre	170	−1.3	29.7	51
Bangladesh	130	0.5	95.5	50
El Salvador	710	−0.2	5.2	64
Turkey	1,240	3.0	47.3	63
Colombia	1,430	3.2	27.5	64
Argentina	2,070	0.5	29.6	70
Brazil	1,880	5.0	129.7	64
Hong Kong	6,000	6.2	5.3	76
United States	14,110	1.7	234.5	75
United Kingdom	9,200	1.7	56.3	74

Source: World Bank

theory, but more widely: this was the age of market-sceptics.

Since the mid-1970s market-optimists have had the upper hand. Many of the new (or revamped) ideas discussed in earlier chapters – for example the market-clearing theories of voluntary un-employment that fit so well with strictures against demand-management – carry the same message. Trust markets; overrule them at your peril. In this respect, said the critics of development econ-omics, the basic economic rules of the game apply as much to poor countries as to rich ones.

Post-war development theory was also attacked from outside the mainstream. To their political objections neo-Marxists added a critique of the idea of gains from trade – the notion that both partners in free trade will gain even if, in absolute terms, one of them makes everything more efficiently than the other. The school fleshed out its dependency theory of economic development to the point where it argued that the L.D.C.s would be better off if they severed ties with the rich north altogether.

Professor Albert Hirschman of Princeton University came up with a simple way to show how the development theories of the 1950s and 1960s were thus trapped in a pincer movement. Two fundamental questions, he says, define the main economic issues. First, does the one true economic theory, whatever it may be, work everywhere? He calls this the mono-economics claim. Second, do rich and poor countries alike gain from trade with each other? That is the mutual-benefit claim.

		Mono-economics?	
		Yes	No
	---	---	---
	Yes	Orthodox economics	Development economics
Mutual benefits?			
	No	Marx?	Neo-Marxist economics

As the matrix above shows, orthodox economists say 'yes' to both. Neo-Marxists say 'no' to both. These two groups then ganged up on a third – the old-school development economists who say 'no' to mono-economics, and 'yes' to mutual benefit. (What about the fellow who says 'yes' to mono-economics, and 'no' to mutual benefit? He is a bit of a puzzle; a classical Marxist, perhaps.)

The parallel between the changes in mainstream theory and the rise and decline of development economics can be taken a stage further. Just as modern Keynesians are stealing what is best in market-clearing macroeconomics and fusing it with their brand of market-realism, development specialists are re-learning the power of price signals, and designing policies that are sensitive to them. They place a new stress on the case-by-case approach, reflecting the enormous diversity of economic conditions in poor countries. To that extent they are not mono-economists. Their common chant, none the less, is that we all obey economic laws – as orthodox economists have been saying for years.

14 Welfare and efficiency

This book has so far dealt with macroeconomics – theories about output, inflation and employment. This chapter looks at the issue of whether and when there are good microeconomic reasons for governments to interfere in free markets.

What is the proper economic role of government? Economists spend much of their time answering that question in terms of macroeconomic policies. But the question can also refer to state intervention in markets – through public spending as well as rules and regulations.

The right framework for analysing government intervention is microeconomics, which studies how an economy allocates resources between different uses, firms and individuals. According to classical microeconomics almost all intervention is unwise. Left to itself, a free-market economy can produce an allocation of resources which is 'Pareto-optimal', a concept named after Vilfredo Pareto, who examined its properties in detail seventy-five years ago. He showed that, on certain assumptions, a free-market economy will allocate resources so that it is impossible to make somebody better off without making somebody else worse off. That is a remarkable result. Adam Smith's invisible hand, working through markets, gathers information about tastes, attitudes, materials and technology, and then combines them in a Pareto-optimal way. No system of central planning could be so efficient. More to the point, any government interference, however modest, removes the guarantee that the economy will reach Pareto efficiency.

Remarkable, yes, but is the Pareto rule much use, when most practical choices involve trade-offs between gainers and losers?

Imagine an island with just two inhabitants. Left to themselves, one gets a monthly income of £1; the other, a diligent exporter, earns £1,000. If they appoint a visiting government from the mainland to tell them what to do, it could tax the high earner and transfer the proceeds until the two islanders each receive £500 a month. Many people would say that the island as a whole is better off with equal shares; according to the Pareto criterion, however, that would not be an improvement (see figure 14.1).

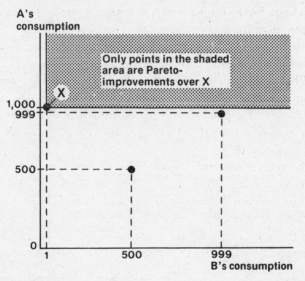

Figure 14.1

In fact, the Pareto criterion would not be satisfied even if the island moved from a £1–£1,000 split to a £999–£999 split. If the government could wave a magic wand and increase total consumption from £1,001 to £1,998, the new state is not a Pareto-improvement on the old: somebody has been made worse off.

To avoid this seeming absurdity, Lord Kaldor and Sir John Hicks proposed a welfare criterion which allowed for the possibility of compensation. If economic growth would allow the gainer to compensate the loser so that collectively they ended up better off, that would be deemed a welfare improvement – whether the compensation took place or not. On this definition, the £999– £999 split does count as an improvement on the £1–£1,000 split – but now the £500–£500 case is actually deemed inferior to £1– £1,000.

The Kaldor–Hicks approach is an improvement over the Pareto criterion in two ways. First, allowing for the possibility of compensation seems to fit better with common sense; it means that increases in national income will always count as welfare gains. Second, it has the technical advantage that it is a far more decisive criterion: given a choice between two patterns of income it will always prefer one over the other, unless they add up to the same total. The Pareto criterion, on the other hand, is indifferent to all those pairs in which there are losers as well as winners; so it has nothing to say in just those cases where policymakers need most guidance.

Unfortunately, the Kaldor–Hicks approach works only by adopting a rule for balancing losses and gains that many find implausible – that an extra £1 does no more to increase the welfare of a poor man than it does to increase the welfare of a rich man. Most government policies of taxing and spending are derived from exactly the opposite belief, so welfare economics is in danger of being dismissed as irrelevant.

What other theories can help guide governments in making choices for society? Some theorists argue that the best guide is the preferences of individuals, so governments ought to count heads and then do what the majority wants. Unfortunately, majority voting has a technical flaw. Suppose three people, A, B and C, have to choose between three alternative policies, X, Y and Z (see table below). Assume that A prefers X to Y and Y to Z. B prefers Y to Z and Z to X. C prefers Z to X and X to Y.

In a vote to choose between X and Y, X will win by two votes to one and in a vote between Y and Z, Y will win by two votes to one. So society prefers X to Y and Y to Z. It should therefore prefer X to Z; in fact, in a vote to choose between X and Z, Z wins by two votes to one.

The paradox of voting

	Voter's order of preference over X, Y, and Z		
Voter	X	Y	Z
A	1	2	3
B	3	1	2
C	2	3	1

Professor Kenneth Arrow of Stanford University has proved that any – literally any – rule for making collective choices will either be inconsistent in this way or else it will fail to satisfy a small set of apparently weak conditions, such as if everybody prefers X to Y, society is deemed to prefer X to Y. Arrow's 'General Impossibility Theorem' shows that a theory of social choice must go beyond theories, such as microeconomics, that are based on individual choice. Free markets do make individual decisions coherent and can guarantee an outcome which is Pareto-efficient, but that outcome has no moral force; and economic theory offers no rules for moving to some socially 'better' outcome.

Markets can fail

Theorists have long stressed that a free-market economy will arrive at Pareto efficiency only if certain assumptions are satisfied. The most important of these is that firms are in perfect competition – i.e. that they are too small to move the market price by themselves; that they have free entry to, and exit from, the industry; and that their customers have perfect information about their goods. These conditions are rarely met in practice. Economists have therefore asked whether departures from perfect competition can justify government intervention.

Take the case of 'natural monopolies'. These are firms which can achieve economies of scale up to or beyond a level of output which is equivalent to the entire industry. Such firms will carry on expanding, to take advantage of lower unit costs, until they are monopolies. Then, of course, they are able to raise their prices and reduce their output in order to boost profits and earn a monopoly rent.

How should a government react to a natural monopoly? One way might be for it to control the monopoly's prices. In this, the government would be guided by a central rule of economic efficiency – that firms set their prices equal to their marginal costs. The price of a good is the value which society puts on consuming an extra unit of it, and the marginal cost is the value of resources needed to produce it.

One response to the monopolist, therefore, is to force him to set his prices equal to his marginal costs. But in the special case of a natural monopoly where unit costs fall as output rises, that will mean forcing the firm to make a loss. If unit costs are falling, it follows arithmetically that the marginal cost of production is less than the unit cost; so setting prices equal to marginal costs will not produce enough revenue to cover the firm's total costs.

This explains why it can make sense to take natural monopolies into the public sector – a private firm would rather go out of business than make a loss. But the problem does not end there. Once the monopoly is under government control it might charge an economically-efficient price and produce the economically efficient quantity, but its financial losses will have to be met from taxes.

Taxation introduces distortions of its own. By taxing goods, the government drives a wedge between price and marginal cost in just the same way as the profit-seeking monopolist does. Consumption will therefore fall to an economically inefficient level, at which the cost of producing one extra unit is less than the value which society places on it.

Economists have long pondered how to reduce the distorting effect of taxation. Modern theorists have couched their ideas in some formidable mathematics, though they have not moved far from a study published in 1927 by Frank Ramsey of Cambridge University. His basic point was simple enough – tax goods which people will want to buy irrespective of price, so that demand will not change.

Figures 14.2 and 14.3 show why that kind of taxation minimizes the economic damage. In figure 14.2, demand for the good rises as its price falls: the D curve is downward sloping. Firms are willing to supply more at higher prices, so the S curve slopes upwards. The curves intersect at point C, where the price is P_1 and the quantity demanded and supplied is Q_1. When the government puts a tax equal to AB on the price of a good, the quantity demanded and supplied falls to Q_2, the price to the firm falls from P_1 to P_F, and the price to the consumer rises from P_1 to P_C.

The shaded area, ABC, is called the deadweight loss of the tax. Society places a value on its consumption equal to the area under the demand curve, so when consumption falls to Q_2, consumers lose welfare equal to the area ACQ_2Q_1. But society also saves some costs by producing less – the savings are shown by the area under the supply curve BCQ_2Q_1. So the loss exceeds the gain by the amount ABC.

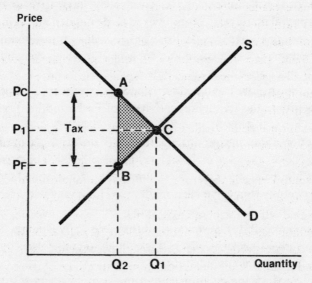

Figure 14.2

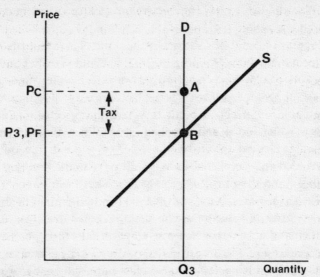

Figure 14.3

In figure 14.3, however, the tax has no effect on the amount demanded, because demand is completely insensitive to price. The optimal amount, Q_3, continues to be demanded and supplied, and there is no deadweight loss. This conclusion justified heavy taxes on goods like alcohol and tobacco, for which demand was largely insensitive to price.

Monopoly power and taxes on goods are two ways that perfect competition, and its theoretical virtue of Pareto-optimality, can fail. This will also happen if buyers and sellers lack full information about the goods they trade. Yet the existence of uncertainty is one of the few certain facts of economic life. For example, sellers almost always know more about their goods than buyers – how carefully they have been made, how long they will last, and how much of the price is accounted for by the makers' costs. Economists call this 'asymmetric information'; by giving sellers a trading advantage over buyers it is enough to nudge the economy away from perfect competition.

But gaps in information can sometimes have more drastic effects; they can cause markets to collapse altogether. Professor

George Akerlof, of the University of California at Berkeley, devised a revealing example of this in a famous paper called 'The Market for Lemons' – not the fruit, but second-hand cars of doubtful quality. Sellers in the second-hand car market have an especially big informational advantage over buyers. When they are selling cars privately – i.e. selling cars that they have used themselves – the sellers know whether they are 'lemons' with patched-up dents and recurring faults, or sound and reliable specimens. The buyers do not.

What effect does this have on the way the market works? One obvious result is that the value of a car drops sharply when it first leaves the distributor's showroom – even if the manufacturer's guarantees can be transferred to subsequent owners. The reason for this is that lemons are scattered randomly through the distributors' stocks, whereas if somebody puts his car back on the market after owning it for only a few months, there is a good chance that he is getting rid of it because it turned out to be a lemon. The car's resale value, which is much lower than would be needed to reflect normal wear and tear, is partly the result of this extra risk of buying a lemon.

More importantly, markets for lemons may sometimes fail to clear altogether. This could happen if, thanks to asymmetric information, falling prices cannot perform their usual market-clearing role of raising demand. Suppose that the best information a buyer has on whether he is buying a lemon is the seller's asking-price. In such a case, when the seller lowers his asking-price he not only makes the good more affordable, he also increases the buyer's estimate of the chance he is buying a lemon. (Most people would hesitate before buying a second-hand car that was offered at much less than the going rate.) If the two effects – affordability versus risk – match each other, the market jams.

Professor Akerlof extended his reasoning to the labour market. The lemons theory might help to explain the existence of involuntary unemployment – the theories discussed in chapters 3 and 8 had to be stretched to account for it. New-classical theorists who think that all unemployment is voluntary argue that any unemployed people who want work will always be able to find it if they only lower their asking-wage enough; if they choose not to, they are really unemployed by choice. But would somebody who offered himself for work at much less than the going rate really find a job so readily? Many buyers would suspect they were being offered the labour-market equivalent of a used car; the further the asking-wage dropped, the more convinced they would be.

Economic games

The buyer's lack of information is only one kind of economic uncertainty. In all its forms, uncertainty plays havoc with the model of perfect competition – and it crops up in some odd places. For example, the problem of monopolistic power can be thought of as another case of uncertainty. Under perfect competition, the firm knows everything it needs to know – it can sell all it makes at the going price. But when a firm, or a group of workers, has market power, it has to take into account the reactions of other actors in the market. A monopolist has to judge how much he will sell if he pushes his prices higher. A trade union has to gauge the effect on employment if it forces wages up.

The logic of 'second guessing' has fascinated economists, particularly since 1944 when John von Neumann and Oskar Morgenstern published *The Theory of Games and Economic Behaviour*. Many of their findings challenged the most cherished assumptions of classical microeconomics.

One of the simplest and most revealing economic 'games' is the 'prisoners' dilemma'. Suppose there are two prisoners, jointly accused of a crime; they face a choice of confessing or not confessing. The prosecutor tells them that if both confess they will go to jail for ten years. If neither owns up, they will get two years for the lesser charge of being present at a crime committed by an unknown villain. But if one confesses and the other does not, the confessor will get a light sentence of one year, while his fellow prisoner goes down for twenty years.

These options can be set out in a 'pay-off' matrix (see below). The matrix shows that the best overall outcome is achieved when both prisoners, A and B, agree not to talk. If they were able to co-operate and agree on a binding contract, they would both keep quiet and receive light punishments. But what if they cannot co-operate? Look at the problem from A's point of view. If B is silent, A is better off if he talks – he goes to jail for only one year instead of two. If B talks, A is again better off if he talks – he goes to jail for ten years instead of twenty. So whatever B decides to do, A is better off if he confesses.

The prisoners' dilemma

	B is silent		B talks	
A is silent	A, 2;	B, 2	A, 20;	B, 1
A talks	A, 1;	B, 20	A, 10;	B, 10

From B's point of view, the problem looks exactly the same. He should confess, rather than keep quiet, too. So the outcome of the game will be that both confess, and go to jail for ten years instead of two. The rational pursuit of individual self-interest does not lead to a socially optimal result.

Psychologists have carried out prisoners'-dilemma experiments (using a system of rewards instead of jail sentences). They found that in repeated trials, the prisoners try to 'communicate' with each other, offering to keep quiet in some trials to see if the other prisoner responds. Sometimes prisoners can feel their way into a keep-quiet agreement and so reach their optimal joint position after all. Such behaviour seems none the less irrational. To see why, remember that on the last trial, there is no economic reason to co-operate with your fellow prisoner – if you confess, he cannot retaliate by confessing in the next trial. So rational prisoners will both confess in the last trial. But if, in the penultimate trial, they know that the other will confess, come what may, in the final trial, it is rational to confess in the penultimate trial, too. Extending this line of reasoning implies that it is rational to confess in every trial.

Does this show that the game theory is wrong? Not at all. It does show that there is more to the idea of rationality than economists usually suppose. True, game theory has disappointed the early hopes of those who thought it would transform economics, partly because the complexity of its more advanced theories discovers ambiguities and uncertainties where classical microeconomics finds elegance and clarity. But game-theory approaches to topics like oligopoly, competitive equilibrium, wage-bargaining and the credibility of government policy are still gaining ground.

Missing markets

Economic theory has focused on one other area where free-market efficiency can break down. A Pareto model assumes that private costs and benefits are equal to social costs and benefits. Often, however, one person's consumption, or one firm's production, will affect others.

Take the example of a house in a street. If you have your house repainted you make your neighbours better off, too; but you will spend no more on repainting than your private balance between costs and benefits dictates. Likewise your neighbours, when they decide how much to spend on maintaining their houses, won't take account of the benefits to you. As a result, your street spends less on painting than would be socially optimal.

House-painting confers external benefits. An example of an external cost is the danger inflicted on other road users when one driver goes too fast. What is missing in both cases is a market through which the externalities can be made to impinge on the decision of how much to consume or produce. As the jargon has it, markets are needed to 'internalize' externalities.

Sometimes, such markets spring up in surprising ways. For years, a favourite textbook example of an externality in production was the story of the bee-keeper and the flower-grower. The bee-keeper's bees help the flower-grower by pollinating his crop; yet he receives no payment, and therefore provides a less-than-efficient amount of pollinating services. This homely tale was ruined when Professor Steven Cheung of the University of Washington decided to check it: he found that flower-growers often do pay fees to local bee-keepers, ensuring a Pareto-optimal amount of buzzing to and fro.

Who compensates whom depends on property rights. For example, a non-smoker who shares an office with a smoker might be willing to pay his room-mate to smoke less. That would be plausible under the convention that people who want to smoke are free to do so. But if the rule were that smokers had to have permission to smoke from their room-mates, shifting the property right to the non-smoker, the smoker would have to pay up. In principle, the socially optimal amount of office smoking would be guaranteed by such compensation (or bribery), regardless of the distribution of rights.

Why do markets not emerge to internalize all externalities, restoring efficiency? First, it may be expensive to establish a market. Suppose a factory is belching smoke, inflicting an external cost on people who live near by. Victims could bribe the factory owner, but it would be difficult and expensive to organize. Second, those who refused to contribute would still get the benefit of the bribe in the form of less smoke – the so-called free-rider problem. Together these factors ensure that market failures will be common.

This seems bad enough, but the problem of missing markets goes even deeper. The pure theory of competitive equilibrium, and its claim of Pareto-optimality, rest on a wider assumption that markets are complete. This does not simply mean that all externalities are internalized. According to Professor Frank Hahn, of Cambridge University, the theory must make 'the unpalatable assumption that there are terms of exchange given for every pair of goods that an individual might wish to exchange'.

To see why that is a very tall order, consider the exact economic meaning of a good. Describing straightforward physical characteristics is not enough: a bar of chocolate available today in London, where it is cold and raining, is not the same thing to buyers and sellers as a bar of chocolate available five years from now in Nairobi, where it will be warm and dry. The pure theory insists that the description of a good must include the time at which it is available, its physical location, and the 'state of nature'. Suppose there are two physical goods, each available at a single point in time and at one location, but in ten different states of the world. Implicitly, the theory then requires twenty (2×10) distinct markets. In reality, only a few of these markets will exist: try getting a quote for that bar-of-chocolate-to-be-available-in-Nairobi-five-years-from-now-if-it's-warm.

Professor Kenneth Arrow of Stanford University has shown how the pure theory might scrape by with fewer markets than this example suggests. Using financial securities, an economy could achieve the same result with twelve markets instead of twenty. There would be two markets for the physical goods, and then ten more for securities; each of the securities traded on those markets would pay out under one particular state of nature, but not under the other nine. Professor Arrow proved that a trader could arrange his affairs with this smaller number of markets exactly as he could with twenty.

This is small comfort. In the real world, there is an infinite number of dates, places and states of nature; only a tiny fraction of the markets needed for the pure theory to hold actually exist. So the competitive model which shows how the invisible hand can achieve Pareto-optimality is doubly unimpressive. First, Pareto-optimal economies are not necessarily desirable – it is easy to think of examples where they are absurdly unjust. Second, the theory in any case is based on assumptions that have little to do with reality. Unfortunately, economists still have little grasp of how governments can nudge the invisible hand in the right direction. So even if the theoretical support for free markets is less strong than it seems, governments might do much more damage if they are too quick to think they know better.

15 What it all adds up to

This final chapter assesses the economic theory, and wonders how economics might change in the next ten years.

Some bits of economic theory have always remained just that – theory, interesting and no doubt clever, but with no practical relevance. Other bits started out as theory but have become the bread and butter of practical economics. The role of prices in affecting both demand and supply is a central theme of all economic analysis, not just among economists but also politicians, businessmen, shoppers and workers. Ask anybody with a market stall how to sell off fruit at the end of the day; his answer will distil the wisdom of generations of economic theorists.

Economics has made progress, producing greater clarity of thought and new evidence on old ideas, but despite these achievements, it remains a quarrelsome subject. To outsiders, the quarrelling proves that economics is at best immature, at worst inherently unreliable. When two intelligent people, both called economists, disagree strongly on issues of major public importance, why take them seriously, let alone allow their subject to guide the fortunes of billions of people?

This impression of unreliability is heightened by the record of economic forecasting. Everybody has his own favourite story of the pundit who ended up with egg on his face. Many of those stories involve economists. Even the most sober research into the achievements of forecasters shows that their errors have often been large, and when they have been right (for example on G.D.P. growth) it has often been for the wrong reasons (for instance because they underestimated consumption but overestimated investment). One study of the forecasts made by the O.E.C.D. in the 1960s concluded that, on most variables, they would have been more accurate if they had simply assumed that last year's figure would be repeated.

What causes these policy disagreements and forecasting errors? Part of the answer to that question lies in the subject matter of economics – millions of markets, billions of transactions, zillions of decisions on how to spend and earn money being made and unmade every day. Economists are always chasing a moving target. The data they can use are from the world as it was, yet are often being used to predict the world as it will be. That is a dangerous leap to make at the best of times; when the world is changing fast and in unexpected ways, it can be fatal. As it happens, the 1970s and 1980s have seen momentous changes of the kind that economics is poorly equipped to handle: rapid inflation, floating exchange rates, the internationalization of financial markets, some huge technological leaps, two oil shocks, the 'debt crisis', the emergence of several economies (Taiwan, South Korea) from peasantry to industrial prosperity. All these happened in a dozen years. No wonder economics has made some mistakes.

Yet it would be wrong to let those mistakes overshadow the positive achievements of economics. Even in such turbulent times, some of the disagreements between economists have been reduced or resolved. It is always hard to judge how much contemporary work on economic theory will be of lasting practical use. But it is already clear that the single most significant theoretical development in the past ten years is moving out of the realm of pure theory. The rational-expectations approach has changed the economic landscape in three main ways. First, it has clarified the crucial part that expectations play in economic models. Second, it has forced modellers to come up with technically better ways of building expectations into their models – the traditional naive equations of backward-looking expectations are no longer acceptable. Third, and much the most important, it has altered the way governments make policy.

Today, all governments understand the need to make their

policies credible. This is not for traditional, 1960s' reasons – such as the danger of disappointing voters by promising too much. Credibility is essential because a disbelieving world will react in ways that undermine everything the policies are supposed to promote. If a government says it will not underwrite higher wages by printing more money, it has to demonstrate that determination for years on end until wage negotiators believe it as surely as they expect night to follow day. If the government behaves erratically, or even says inconsistent things, it is signalling to wage negotiators that they might get away with a big increase without the penalty of bankruptcy or unemployment.

This emphasis on expectations has dictated economic policy in several countries. In the United States in 1981, President Reagan announced a three-year programme of cuts in personal taxes, hoping that people would then not want to treat their extra income as a windfall and save it. Governments in most industrial countries now index their tax systems against inflation, so that people are no longer surprised at every budget by a 'rise' in indirect taxes or a 'cut' in income tax. The same spirit underlies the 'medium-term financial strategy' which Britain's Conservative government introduced in 1980. It wanted to create a climate of stable expectations about its plans. It tried to do this by announcing four-year targets for monetary growth and public borrowing.

The new attitude is not confined to those who are misleadingly called 'monetarists'. Many new Keynesians, like Professor James Meade of Cambridge University, accept the merits of pre-announced targets for the main economic variables. Professor Meade prefers aggregate demand (G.D.P. in money terms) to monetary growth, but the principle is similar. The new Keynesians in Britain tend to argue that the Thatcher government misunderstood the true insight of rational-expectations theory, and therefore tried to move too quickly. If its counter-inflationary policies had been more gradualist, it would have done less damage to output and jobs while still succeeding in bringing inflation down to about 5 per cent by the mid-1980s.

Whatever the rights and wrongs of that particular argument, one more important point stands out. Few economists now believe that governments can or should 'fine-tune' demand. The whole vocabulary of fine-tuning – 'pushing the accelerator', 'a touch on the brake' – has barely been used in academic circles for ten years. Yet in the 1960s, economists used to spend weeks on end working out whether the government should add £250m to demand, or £280m; those who wanted the Chancellor to put his foot down hard would daringly plump for £300m.

That way of thinking is dead, its death a tribute to the power of the rational-expectations approach. It raises an interesting question about the links between ideas, policy and economic performance. Suppose that some theorists come up with a new idea about how the economy works. It is so persuasive that policymakers start to follow its prescriptions – and everybody believes that they will indeed do so. Will not that change by itself alter the way the economy works? And if it does, will it thereby cease to be a helpful guide for policymakers, since it had been derived from (and was therefore relevant to) the earlier performance of the economy? In short, ideas might be able to change economic variables, making the problem of aiming at a moving target even more tricky than suggested earlier in this chapter.

There is one other area where economists have reached a new consensus of considerable practical importance. They agree that economies have a supply side. That seems so obvious a statement as to be not worth saying. Yet twenty years ago, the idea of an aggregate-supply curve (described in chapters 3 and 8) had no place in economics textbooks. Its emergence and widespread acceptance have helped to highlight the factors that cause unemployment. Most economists now agree on the list of possible causes. Any disagreements they have arise over (a) which are the most important causes – an empirical question that is still far from being settled; and (b) which causes should be tackled and by what methods. This last is mainly a political question concerning, for example, the legal rights and privileges of trade unions, or the social desirability of a minimum wage.

The political divide

The fact that economists disagree about politics might seem no more surprising than that some engineers vote for left-wing parties and others for right-wing ones. Yet it helps to explain why economics seems so disputatious even though it has settled several subjects that used to be hotly contested. In truth, there is no such thing as 'pure economics', a straightforward science with right or wrong answers. Its original title, political economy, is still a better guide to its nature.

The political content of most economics is large enough to allow two types of distortions to affect the subject. First, non-economists can categorize disagreements between economists in familiar political terms. If Professor X happens to see a link between monetary growth now and price inflation two years later, then he is a monetarist; monetarism is then quickly equated with a belief in market forces and an indifference to high un-employment; in no time at all, Professor X is being branded as favouring capital punishment and flogging in schools. In the public mind, economic debate consists of monetarism versus Keynesianism – irreconciled and irreconcilable.

This glib interpretation is encouraged by the second distortion, which is created by economists themselves. They have made remarkable progress in agreeing on the significance of rational-expectations theory and the existence of a supply curve. Yet they obscure these agreements because they (like many other people) enjoy a good political argument. The heart of that argument, for them as for others, is about the proper role of government. To simplify with labels, liberals believe that most governmental powers are a threat to individual liberty and should therefore be restricted as far as possible. By contrast, social democrats believe that governments should intervene in many areas to protect liberties, correct market failures and promote social justice.

Neither of these beliefs is provable in any scientific sense. Yet both impinge on a range of issues to which economists apply their minds. To take one example, personal taxation is a subject that all economists have views about. Some think that a progressive tax system damages incentives; others say that, on the contrary, it encourages highly-paid people to earn even more so as to maintain their standard of living. The empirical evidence is ambiguous enough to support both points of view. Yet suppose that it was suddenly transformed by numerous studies showing that high marginal tax rates had no disincentive effects at all. It is hard – nay, impossible – to imagine that every liberal economist would suddenly drop his opposition to progressive taxes. Believing what you like believing is a powerful human quality. In the jargon it is called 'cognitive dissonance'. Economics has a lot of it.

The technical divide

The big dividing line in economics today is between new classicals and new Keynesians. The policy issues that divide them have been described in this book. But it is not only what they think; it is also how they think. Their whole approach to economic theorizing and their choice of what to study is different. The first priority of the new-classical economists is theoretical rigour. Most of their papers are highly mathematical; their arguments are austere and formal. Keynesians usually prefer relevance. Their papers are more obviously at pains to address real, rather than hypothetical, issues – though 'reality' is, of course, partly in the eye of the beholder. To take one example, there may be some theoretical difficulties in the idea of involuntary unemployment; but Keynesians see plenty of it about, so they ask what policies might reduce it.

This dispute about methodology can be illustrated by an axiom favoured by Professor Milton Friedman. In a celebrated article, he argued that it does not matter if the assumptions of an economic model are unrealistic. What matters is that the model is logically consistent, and that it accurately predicts the things you want it to predict. The new-classical economists agree. They are therefore unworried by criticisms of their assumption that markets clear.

The new-Keynesian approach also has its critics. For example some Keynesians make assumptions about, wage-setting behaviour which may seem realistic, yet can be hard to reconcile with the idea of rationality that underpins the Keynesian model. New Keynesians reply that they are happy to tolerate such technical inconsistencies in exchange for greater relevance.

Because the new-classical economists prefer more formal methods of reasoning, they have made greater use of mathematics. Economists of all persuasions suspect that is one reason why the new classical school has attracted so many young supporters, particularly in the United States. They enjoy the sheer intellectual pleasure of advanced maths. And – market forces at work – there are many fewer jobs for pure mathematicians than for economists, so the clever mathematician switches to economics.

The new-Keynesian school now has more to offer the mathematically-inclined than it did a dozen years ago. Here are four areas where hard mathematics and Keynesian 'relevance' can go hand-in-hand.

Keynesian models with rational expectations

One of the most active areas of current research is the analysis of models that assume rational expectations, but still leave a role for government policy to stabilize the economy. One such group of models is based on the idea of overlapping contracts in labour markets. If different groups of workers reach pay agreements at different times of the year, wages in the aggregate can change in response to a shock, like a change in government policy, but slowly. The response will be lagged by the complex structure of contracts, even if workers correctly alter their expectations of future inflation. Nominal wages lag behind prices, just as if expectations were backward-looking. The maths is fun; the results are Keynesian.

Game theory

This branch of mathematical economics has disappointed some of the early hopes for it. Progress has been slow because of its technical demands. The simplest two-person games – such as the prisoners' dilemma discussed in the previous chapter – are easy enough. Three-person games are far harder to manipulate. And to apply game-theory methods to the analysis of competitive equilibrium, for example, can be fiendishly difficult.

However, these techniques are now attracting more interest. Coincidentally, the debate between new-Keynesian and new-classical economics highlighted two issues that are particularly suitable for game-theory treatment. First, the theory of labour markets and wage determination is concerned with a bargaining process that comes straight from the game theorist's handbook. Second, the fashion for monetary targets puts governments in a strategic game with trade unions and other interest groups. How far should the government's commitments be binding if these groups decide to call its bluff?

The theory of the second best

A student's biggest disappointment in learning microeconomics has long been the fact that the familiar efficiency rules – e.g. setting price equal to marginal cost – can all fail if only one of them is broken. The previous chapter discussed the case of natural monopolies, and explained that setting price equal to marginal cost enhanced economic efficiency, even though it forced the monopoly to make a loss. But that assumes that, everywhere else in the economy, competitive firms are setting their prices equal to marginal cost, too. The theory of the second best proved that if that condition did not hold, the monopoly would need some other pricing rule. The search for rules when policy can only make the best of a bad job still has far to go.

The theory of social choice

Formal logic is the branch of mathematics that has proved most useful in this theorizing. Professor Amartya Sen of Oxford University has pioneered the approach in his book *Collective Choice in Social Welfare*. The challenge is to examine the relationship between (a) a society's objectives on such things as the distribution of income and (b) the individual preferences of the people who make up the society. How far is it possible to tie collective decisions to individual choices?

These examples show that mathematics is not the exclusive property of any particular school of economic thought. As a result, the attractions of new-classical economics for students seeking a technical challenge may start to weaken – though even Keynesians find little comfort in that if they come from the generation which favours analysis through words. To such people, the spread of mathematics into every corner of economics is itself the biggest worry.

The drift towards greater use of mathematics is none the less unstoppable. Nor is that necessarily a bad thing. Economics will always need, and have, its communicators and power-seekers – those who would rather move events in the world than symbols on paper. They will continue to explain the frontiers of mathematical progress to puzzled policymakers. As long as there are ways for less worldly economists to clarify issues through new uses of mathematics, the study of economics will carry on.

Empirical cul-de-sac

How much progress is left to be made? On the theoretical side of economics, it is safe to say that some of the biggest developments have already happened. A hundred years hence, textbooks will surely still give pride of place to notions like marginal cost and marginal revenue – which had not even been invented a hundred years ago. Having said that, many areas of theoretical economics remain relatively unexplored.

On the empirical side, however, there are already signs that researchers have reached a point of sharply diminishing returns. They continue to pile on the effort and the computer-time, but their ability (a) to test theories statistically and (b) to build models for forecasting makes slower and slower progress. Econometricians test theories by asking how well they fit the statistical evidence from the real world. The technical problems are enormous, because reliable tests can be carried out only if the data meet a series of requirements. That means econometricians have to test their tests, to ensure that they do not accept a theory that they should reject, or vice versa.

The more advanced this operation becomes, the wider the gap between the theory of theory-testing and the practice of economics. The practitioners – economists in finance ministries, central banks and private businesses, as well as in universities – know that the basic data are often badly measured in the first place and then subject to frequent and large revisions. To take one example, in the mid-1980s the world's balance of payments contains a 'residual' of roughly $100 billion a year on current account. The surpluses and deficits of different countries simply do not sum to zero. Yet thousands of hours of computer-time are spent analysing whether the United States deficit will be $125 billion or $130 billion. The econometric techniques used are brilliant, no doubt, but they are also beside the point. That is why more practical economists are happy to rely on statistical methods that were available twenty years ago.

Using models to make forecasts, rather than to represent the world as it is, faces extra problems of its own. First among these is the now-notorious Lucas critique – the fact that a change in government policy can alter the entire structure of an economic model, not just those bits where the policy features explicitly. Hence it is wrong to use econometric models to answer questions such as 'how much will an increase in government spending affect business investment after two years?'. Modellers, of course, have carried on regardless; they accept the Lucas critique in principle, but argue that it may not matter much in practice.

Advances in forecasting have been disappointing in other ways. An alliance between mathematics and computer technology has meant that models can grow and grow. The large models used by governments and, increasingly, by small and medium-sized private forecasting firms now contain many hundreds of equations. They are bigger; are they better? In many ways, no. First, comparisons have shown that giant models are often worse at forecasting key variables like inflation and output than much smaller models. One approach with a good forecasting record avoids economics altogether, and forecasts variables solely on the basis of their previous values. Second, large models are so complex that their users lose all 'feel' for what is going on inside the equations. That makes it harder to judge their results. Third, in spite of their size, large models can be easily upset by small changes in their design. A model with 1,000 equations might be changed from Keynesian to new classical by altering one or two equations.

Size does not bring certainty. Its only real advantage is that it provides a forecast which is detailed enough to please the small print of policy – which taxes to change, which spending programmes to revise, and so on. Details matter, of course. But economics should never lose sight of the big intellectual questions; in some areas, it is starting to.

Progress to come

Although it is hazardous to guess the next big intellectual breakthroughs in economics, this book will end with two tentative suggestions. The first is the behaviour of government itself, the second is the whole idea of rationality.

To start with government. Most of the big theoretical advances in macroeconomics have come from 'endogenizing the exogenous' – explaining things that had previously been taken as given. In the 1930s, John Maynard Keynes did this for employment. Until then, classical economics had simply taken it for granted that labour markets were either in, or heading for, full-employment equilibrium. At the height of the Great Depression, a distinguished continental economist was asked to deliver a guest lecture at the London School of Economics. With the British jobless rate well into double figures, he began his discourse with the words 'Assume full employment'.

The same endogenizing has happened to expectations. Keynes was the first to see how important guesses about the future could be for economics. He emphasized their role in the *General Theory*, and many of his later interpreters rated that one of the book's most important innovations. But Keynes had no theory of how expectations were formed. Instead of developing a model that worked them out endogenously – simultaneously with other variables in the economy – he assumed they were fixed in the short run. Later generations of economists, unhappy with this treatment, gnawed away at the problem until some produced the rational-expectations theory that has transformed large parts of macroeconomics.

Something similar is happening to international trade. Forecasting models for individual economies used to assume that world trade would grow by a figure plucked from the air. Now they accept that their own economy's performance will affect world trade, eventually feeding back to change domestic performance. International linkages – in finance as well as trade – are much in vogue.

The next candidate for endogenizing may well be the government. Several prominent theorists, mainly in America, are analysing government spending with similar tools to those they would use on private consumption or investment. They see government policies as being driven in a predictable way by economic and political variables, most of which can be quantified and then used for forecasting purposes. The approach is known as the theory of 'public choice'. Given its subject matter, if it can make a breakthrough, it will be a big one.

Rationality is the second area where theorists might produce significant advances in understanding economic behaviour. Almost all economic theory assumes that people are rational in a very specific sense: they try to maximize their welfare based solely on a lifetime of consuming goods – these include leisure and, arguably, the 'good' of making bequests. Managers of firms are 'rational' too – they try to maximize their profits. Yet the details of this rational behaviour have seldom been explored. One man who has done so is Professor Gary Becker of Chicago University. He has tirelessly analysed the economic rationale for decisions like getting married or having children. Sentimental types may think they make these choices for reasons that have little or nothing to do with economics. Not so, says Professor Becker: he finds a good statistical explanation for their behaviour.

Other theorists are exploring rationality in a different way. Instead of applying the economist's narrow definition of rationality to a broader set of problems – the Becker approach – they are broadening the notion of rationality to explain behaviour that seems deeply irrational to the conventional economist.

For example, Professor George Akerlof of the University of California at Berkeley has based economic models on the idea of 'cognitive dissonance' – psychologists' jargon for the everyday phenomenon of believing what you want to believe. Professor Akerlof quotes psychologists' findings that workers in nuclear plants often refuse to wear their safety equipment, because they prefer not to think that their job is dangerous.

Note that this is not necessarily 'irrational' behaviour; the workers might well be maximizing their happiness subject to the constraint that they have to do the work they do. But the idea goes beyond traditional microeconomic theory: it says that people not only make choices about what to consume, they also make choices about what to believe. Models like this can provide new grounds for government intervention in pursuit of society's rational goals – in the nuclear workers' case, for example, the government might devise and enforce safety rules.

This kind of work hints at a new and challenging direction for economics. Professor Robert Solow, reviewing Professor Akerlof's attempts to draw in assumptions from a range of non-economic social sciences, said his studies 'show how much good can come from combining skilful economic analysis with a willingness to take seriously the elementary facts of social life'. Up to now, only a few economists have done more than pay lip-service to that ideal.

Such research could lead anywhere. But, if it catches on, one aspect is bound to be reassuringly familiar. Trawling the wide oceans of the other social sciences will guarantee a limitless supply of phrases like 'cognitive dissonance'; jargon will always be the life-blood of the professional economist.

Suggestions for further reading

We tried to make this book accessible to novices, but because we also aimed for brevity, some readers will have found the going heavy in parts. Such readers might want to try a slower approach to economic theory, starting from the first principles of elementary supply and demand analysis. Others – the majority, we hope – will want to go more deeply into some of the theories we have discussed. They must consult books which are more exhaustive, more rigorous, and, unfortunately, more difficult than this one. Here is a guide to both sorts of further reading.

A word of warning. The progress of modern economic theory is recorded in technical journals like the *American Economic Review*, the *Economic Journal*, and *Econometrica*. Twenty years ago many of the articles in such journals were accessible to intelligent laymen who could face up to jargon. No longer. Much of this material is now highly mathematical; readers without a strong technical background – and that means a fairly recent economics degree – will be out of their depth.

With a couple of exceptions, the readings we recommend here are not from the journals. Instead we review a wide range of books, from those that assume absolutely no economic training, to those which take at least some preparation, including a smattering of mathematics, for granted. (We say which is which.) Those who really do want to grapple with the cutting edge of the economics profession will find ample references to the journals in these books.

General economics textbooks

Paul Samuelson's *Economics* (McGraw Hill, 1948, 1985) is deservedly the most famous of all introductory economics books. Now in its twelfth edition, it has introduced hundreds of thousands of students to the subject – many more than any other book. Generations of readers have seen it change substantially through the years, and now quarrel over which edition is best; revisions have reflected theoretical developments and, to a smaller extent, changing fashions over which parts of the subject matter most. In all this, the strength of the book comes from a combination that others find hard to match. Samuelson is one of the top three or four living economic theorists, with major developments in most branches of the subject, not to mention a Nobel prize, to his name; so he lacks nothing in authority. Yet he is also a careful teacher; his book is well planned, and written in a lively and readable style. It calls for no preparation except an interest in the issues.

There must be twenty or thirty clones of Samuelson's book. Until recently the only strong challenger – especially for British readers, for whom its examples are tailored – was Richard Lipsey's *Introduction to Positive Economics* (Weidenfeld and Nicolson, 1963). It is as clear as Samuelson, but not as much fun. The newcomer that poses the most serious threat to the master is *Economics*, by Stanley Fischer and Rudiger Dornbusch (McGraw Hill, 1983). These professors from the Massachusetts Institute of Technology are among the brightest of that generation of American theorists who have yet to win a Nobel prize but are no longer merely promising. Both have made substantial contributions to theory. Their book is as lucid as Samuelson's, and as careful to link discussion of principles to the real world. It is more successful in the way it integrates recent theories with traditional material.

The names of Fischer and Dornbusch now appear on a British version of their textbook, but after that of David Begg. The ordering is fair. Mr Begg, of Worcester College, Oxford, has done much more than change all the dollar signs to pounds. His version is a different and, in many respects, even better book – particularly in the way it gives the reader occasional tastes of advanced new theories, free of the heavy-duty mathematics that generally encumbers them.

The books by Begg, Dornbusch and Fischer are still in the Samuelson, one-volume-tells-all mould. They cover elementary microeconomics as well as the macroeconomic theory that has been the preoccupation of this book. Readers who start with a special interest in macro-policy – the link between money and prices, the effects of budget deficits, the causes of unemployment, and so on – might not want to wade through two or three hundred pages of microeconomics first; they might also want a deeper treatment of the macro-issues than these basic texts provide. There is no reason why such readers should not try an intermediate-level macroeconomics book instead. Contrary to the established textbook pattern, you do not need micro to learn macro; for all but very advanced students the two branches are taught as quite separate subjects, as linguists might study French and German. Most practising macroeconomists have forgotten what little microeconomics they ever knew.

William Branson's *Macroeconomic Theory and Policy* (Harper and Row, 1972) is the outstanding book in this category. Harder than the Samuelsons of this world, it is aimed – according to the preface – at senior undergraduates and postgraduate students. It gives a detailed explanation of the individual models of consumption, investment, and the markets for money and labour; these are the building blocks of the simplest economic model that is any use for thinking about policy. It also looks at the medium-term dynamics of stock adjustment (deficits and all that), and longer-term growth. The presentation is mathematical, which allows it to be concise and rigorous, but the maths is not hard. Readers need nothing fancier than the elementary calculus they should have learned by the fourth year of secondary school. The book is crystal-clear – especially the preliminary chapters that describe the basic IS–LM model – so it is an excellent bridge to the original literature and the frontiers of economics.

A book worth considering as an alternative, or supplement, to Branson's is Robert Barro's *Macroeconomics* (Wiley, 1984). Professor Barro set out to write an introductory book that approached macroeconomics from the new-classical perspective, rather than in the amended-Keynesian tradition of IS–LM. His book therefore builds on the unKeynesian notion of continuously clearing markets, and gives special attention to the role of rational expectations in each part of the economy. The book is easier than Branson's, but only because it avoids trickier issues its section on economic growth, for example, is far too brief.

Macroeconomic Topics

The theory of rational expectations has reshaped modern economics; it is worth seeking out books devoted to explaining what the theory is and what it is not. This time, David Begg's name is the only one on the cover of *The Rational Expectations Revolution in Macroeconomics* (Philip Allan, 1982). The book is hard in places, because it shirks no complications. Three sections which are intelligible only to the mathematically robust (including a whole chapter on the implications of rational expectations for econometric testing) are starred; most of the book uses elementary mathematical notation. It therefore succeeds in making the most advanced technical papers accessible to undergraduate-level students.

Note, though, that Mr Begg is an 'eclectic Keynesian'; he debunks some of the more extravagant claims made for the theory. *Rational Expectations and the New Macroeconomics* by Patrick Minford and David Peel (Martin Robertson, 1983) has no such reservations. Mr Minford runs the econometric model at Liverpool University – the only one in Britain that has wholeheartedly adopted the new-classical approach. This book, too, is up-to-date on the technical literature and, as a result, hard for those with little preparation.

A better book for the beginner, or for somebody whose

economics degree dates from an earlier era, might be *Rational Expectations: Macroeconomics for the 1980s* by Michael Carter and Rodney Maddock (Macmillan, 1984). The authors make no claim to have written a comprehensive survey of the literature; they try instead to make the main ideas accessible to beginners and non-economists. They spared the maths, and produced a short, readable book.

There are other branches of economic theory where broad textbooks like Branson's cannot really do justice to recent research. The theory of monetary policy has been at the centre of enormous controversy inside and outside the economics profession; politicians with but the faintest grasp of the issues have at different times denounced or pledged allegiance to 'monetarism'. Readers can pursue this trail in several ways.

Victoria Chick's *Theory of Monetary Policy* (Basil Blackwell, 1977) is based on a set of lectures given to her final-year undergraduates at University College, London. It gives a clear and concise survey of the field as it stood by the mid-1970s, managing to find good and bad things to say about every school of thought. A technical book, it assumes familiarity with intermediate-level texts like Branson's. Ms Chick starts by referring to a lively debate between James Tobin, Milton Friedman, Karl Brunner, Allan Meltzer and others, published as a symposium in the September 1972 issue of the *Journal of Political Economy*. (The papers were also published in book form in 1974 by the Chicago University Press under the title *Milton Friedman's Monetary Framework* edited by Robert Gordon.) This is a classic confrontation – one exception to our no-journals rule, and an antidote, as Ms Chick says, for those who think there is nothing to discuss in monetary theory.

The empirical side of the monetary policy debate is also of great interest. The Treasury and Civil Service Committee of the House of Commons has done students a service here. In the early 1980s the committee conducted an inquiry into the Thatcher administration's 'medium-term financial strategy' – monetarism in action, as many at the time supposed. As part of this exercise it sent dozens of the leading economists in Britain and America a questionnaire on monetary policy, asking what the connection is between money and prices, between interest rates and money, between the government's budget deficit and interest rates, between interest rates and the exchange rate, and so on. Many of the academics refused to answer those questions, and submitted answers to their own instead (do they let their students do this?). Their replies have been published in two volumes of *Monetary Memoranda* (HMSO, 1980).

The Federal Reserve Bank of New York and the Bank of England have both published books which are helpful to monetary students. The New York Fed's *U.S. Monetary Policy and Financial Markets*, written by Paul Meek (1982), is about monetary policy as seen from the 'vantage point of the trading desk where domestic open-market operations are carried out'. Aimed at non-economists, it is clear and well written. The price is right, too; it's free to anybody who writes to the Fed's information office and asks for it.

The Bank of England's *Development and Operation of Monetary Policy 1960–1983* (1984) is a collection of articles from the Bank's Quarterly Bulletin. Connecting passages weave these extracts into a continuous story that covers the period after the Radcliffe Report, through the experiment known as Competition and Credit Control, to the years since 1976 when targets for monetary growth began to be publicly announced. The tone is dry; objections to thinking at the Treasury – the Bank's formal master on most of these issues – are so deeply coded that non-bureaucrats may miss them. But there is no better reference to the twists and turns of monetary policy in Britain.

Apart from Robert Barro's introductory textbook, the leaders of the new-classical school have made little attempt to reach non-specialists: the published work of men like Robert Lucas and Thomas Sargent is formidably technical. Fortunately, Arjo Klamer has given us *The New Classical Macroeconomics: Conversations with New Classical Economists and Their Opponents* (Wheatsheaf Books, 1983). His book is a collection of interviews, printed verbatim. He talked to Lucas and Sargent, to their ardent young follower Robert Townsend, to critics like James Tobin, Franco Modigliani, and Robert Solow, and to new Keynesians of the younger generation like Alan Blinder.

Mr Klamer's project might easily have satisfied nobody – too shallow to help the specialist, too full of jargon to mean anything to newcomers. In fact, the book is an unqualified success, fascinating on several levels. Mr Klamer asks the right questions, and forces each of his victims to clarify their views on the vital – and usually obscure – points of contention. It emerges, for example, that the theory of rational expectations has been used by new classicists as a Trojan horse for their logically separate market-clearing approach. But the book is just as interesting for the light it casts on the nature of academic economists – and on the social and intellectual pressures that shape their views.

James Tobin attacks the new classical school at greater length in his austerely titled *Asset Accumulation and Economic Activity* (Basil Blackwell, 1980), four lectures delivered in Helsinki in 1978. One lecture focuses on the so-called neo-Ricardian idea that rational expectations of future taxes mean that government-debt sales have no real economic effects. Another shows how standard IS–LM analysis can take into account the effects of the government's budget deficit, and other shifts in stocks of assets, and still arrive at broadly Keynesian conclusions about the effects of fiscal and monetary policy. Simply written, it is a readable and elegant little book.

The post-war Keynesian consensus has lately had to fight off attacks from another direction. The supply-side revolution has been vastly overblown, but behind the hype are some important ideas. Lafferites, including Laffer and supply-siders of a less virulent strain, speak for themselves in *The Supply-Side Solution*, edited by Bruce Bartlett and Timothy Roth (Chatham House Publications, 1983). This volume goes well beyond the economically empty rhetoric of earlier efforts, though it still focuses on a fairly narrow issue – the effect of tax changes on incentives to save and invest.

Michael Evans's *The Truth About Supply-Side Economics* (Basic Books, 1983) examines the same issue, but is more persuasive because it is better balanced. It starts by explaining why four of the school's tenets failed in America after 1980. These myths were: interest rates would fall as soon as the President announced his 1981 tax cuts; tight money and fiscal laxity would generate balanced growth; lower business taxes would increase investment at once; Reaganomics would balance the federal budget. But then Mr Evans defends the valid core of the supply-side approach: lower taxes can lead to higher savings, better productivity, and faster growth.

Lawrence Klein, the Nobel prize-winning Keynesian, argues for a broader supply-side perspective in his recent book, *The Economics of Supply and Demand* (Basil Blackwell, 1983). His view of supply-side issues is in tune with this book's chapters on supply factors – the traditional preoccupation with demand-side factors can lead economic models seriously astray; economics should pay more attention to the markets for labour and for other factors of production, including human skills. One chapter shows how an econometric model can simulate the effects of higher oil prices on the world economy.

An important book that focuses more narrowly on the labour market is James Meade's *Wage-Fixing* (George Allen & Unwin, 1982), the first volume of a two-part study, *Stagflation*. Professor Meade stresses that measures to expand aggregate demand will only succeed if the labour market translates extra demand into higher output instead of higher inflation. To improve its ability to do that, he suggests radical reforms in (Britain's) wage-fixing institutions, including a statutory incomes policy backed up by anti-inflation taxes and marginal employment subsidies, and compulsory arbitration in wage disputes with a duty on the arbitrators to take employment effects into account. Meanwhile, financial policies would be aimed at maintaining gentle growth in aggregate demand. (The second volume, *Demand Management*, written with David Vines and Jan Maciejowski, looks at this in more detail.) Mathematics is relegated to appendices, making for a rare book: state-of-the-art economics, influential with policymakers, and accessible to non-economists.

Finally under this heading, three excellent books that do not fit readily into any of our slots. First, *The Role and Limits of Government* (Temple Smith, 1983), by Samuel Brittan. The author is the chief economics commentator of the *Financial Times*; his weekly columns are influential in Britain's policymaking circles. The essays in this book range from theoretical aspects of monetarism and Keynesianism (the volume includes a rewritten version of his classic pamphlet, 'How to End the Monetarist Controversy'), the problems of economic policy in Britain and America, to abstract questions of political philosophy. On many of these matters Mr Brittan takes a refreshingly independent stance.

Second, George Akerlof's *An Economic Theorist's Book of Tales* (Cambridge, 1984). This short collection of papers includes the studies on markets for 'lemons' (mentioned in chapter 14) and on the economic effects of cognitive dissonance (mentioned in chapter 15). They represent an unconventional approach to economic theory, which Mr Akerlof sums up as the 'willingness to entertain the consequences of new assumptions'. The paper on lemons sparked a literature on asymmetric information that has affected microeconomic and macroeconomic thinking in important ways, and the collection as a whole may signpost a future course for economic theory. Most of the papers use little mathematics – and it is usually assigned to appendices.

Third, Arthur Okun's *Prices and Quantities* (Basil Blackwell, 1981). Mr Okun died at the peak of his intellectual powers in 1980. In this book, published shortly after his death, he attacked the notion of short-run flexibility in wages and prices – a cornerstone of most traditional models – and synthesized recent research on implicit contracts, job-search models, and expectations. The book is as much about the microeconomics of markets as about macroeconomic policy; such a lucid melding of the two branches of economics is virtually unique. Though Mr Okun was technically sharp, there is no mathematics in the book; the arguments are in beautifully written English.

International economics

The treatment of international trade and capital flows is often another gap in the one-volume textbooks. Branson's, for example, gives the issue one twenty-six-page chapter – enough only to show how the IS–LM model can be expanded to represent a simple open economy. That leaves no room to review, or even mention, the numerous competing theories of exchange rates and the balance of payments.

For this, two other recent books are better. John Williamson's *The Open Economy and the World Economy* (Basic Books, 1983) is an up-to-date version of the traditional international economics textbook. It covers the microeconomics of comparative advantage and gains from trade, protection and resource allocation; it also has detailed chapters on the macroeconomics of trade, balance-of-payments and exchange-rate theories, and government policy in the open economy. It is especially good at making theory relevant to policy issues – Mr Williamson's speciality as a fellow of Washington's Institute for International Economics (see below). The book is hard in places – for this blame the subject, which is often unavoidably tricky – but it is well written and has a very modern feel.

Victor Argy's *The Postwar International Money Crisis* (George Allen & Unwin, 1981) adds occasional obscurities in presentation to the intrinsic difficulty of its subject. But it is worth considering as an alternative to Williamson's book because it skips the microeconomics of trade to concentrate on setting out the history of the international economy. A good half of the book is a concise and fairly mathematical review of recent theories of international macroeconomics. Mr Argy assumes that his readers already know quite a lot.

A book on international economic theory that is more rigorous – and much harder – than Argy's is Rudiger Dornbusch's *Open Economy Macroeconomics* (Basic Books, 1980). Mr Dornbusch was the earliest architect of models that had the property of exchange-rate overshooting; his book is now a standard text for advanced undergraduates and postgraduate students. The publisher's blurb is right, for once, to call it pathbreaking; but it is for the economically and mathematically sophisticated only.

For those who want a fuller history of the practice of international economics, with less theory, there are two good choices. First, Robert Solomon's *The International Monetary System, 1945–81* (Harper and Row, 1982). This is as much a memoir as a history, because Mr Solomon helped to formulate American economic policy during the 1960s and 1970s, a period of drastic change in the international economy. His book gives a good idea of the factors that undermined and finally crushed the Bretton Woods regime. Robert Aliber's *The International Money Game* (Macmillan, 1983) looks at the same issues, but organizes them thematically rather than chronologically. As its demotic title suggests, it is aimed at the non-specialist, and is particularly good at decoding jargon.

To stay on top of the latest international economic developments, keep an eye on the occasional policy studies published by the Institute for International Economics – a Washington thinktank which has maintained a steady flow of top-quality analysis. The series includes John Williamson's *The Exchange Rate System* (1983), and Ronald McKinnon's *An International Standard for Monetary Stabilization* (1984). Stephen Marris, another fellow of the institute, took part in a recent symposium on the foreign-exchange value of the dollar organized by the Brookings Institution – along with Jeffrey Frankel, Richard Cooper, Rudiger Dornbusch, and James Tobin. Their papers and a summary of their discussion have been published in the *Brookings Papers on Economic Activity, 1985*, volume 1. Not too technical; well worth looking up.

Development economics and growth theory

Three of the most interesting new books on development economics look back over the past thirty years of practice and research, and try to say where this branch of economics now stands. A new collection of essays edited by Gerald Meier and Dudley Seers, *Pioneers in Development* (World Bank, 1985), is an excellent first book for newcomers. It includes papers by Arthur Lewis, Raúl Prebisch, Peter Bauer, H. W. Singer, Albert Hirshmann, Gunnar Myrdal and other leading lights. Paul Streeten, Michael Lipton, Bela Balassa and others offer their comments. The papers vary in style. Some are personal memoirs of formative years, others informal accounts of the changes development economics has seen since the 1940s – which ideas still stand up, which have had to be revised or shelved. These men have reputations to protect; but the book as a whole gives a well-balanced picture.

Another new book – *Investing in Development: Lessons of World Bank Experience*, by Warren Baum and Stokes Tolbert (World Bank, 1985) – echoes many of the same themes. The authors, senior Bank officials, tell the story of growing disillusionment with industrialization as the key to development, and of the importance of raising the efficiency of farming. They are more honest than some of the illuminati over what went wrong in the past, and admit to some painful planning errors.

Ian Little's *Economic Development* (Basic Books, 1982) is also preoccupied with the lessons of history, but this is a broader survey of basic development theory, as well as policy on aid, planning, export promotion, and reliance on market signals. In common with the book by Baum and Tolbert, it is happy with the idea of development economics as a separate discipline (or, as chapter 13 puts it, it rejects the mono-economics claim), but it none the less welcomes many of the free-market insights that have undermined the special status of the subject in recent years.

The man who has argued most fiercely against the planning approach to development is Peter Bauer, the field's leading conservative economist. *Equality, the Third World, and Economic Delusion* (Methuen, 1982) is a recent and representative collection of essays in defence of liberal economic theory. One brilliantly-argued paper attacks the idea that population growth has held back economic development in the poor countries; others argue that foreign aid usually does more harm than good to most people in the countries that receive it. Mr Bauer set out a concise statement of his controversial views on aid in an article (co-written with Basil Yamey) in the September 1985 issue of *Commentary*; put simply, he thinks that aid does not work because it rewards economic failure.

Albert Hirschman's *Essays in Trespassing* (Cambridge University Press, 1981) includes his paper 'The Rise and Decline of Development Economics', which was mentioned in chapter 13. It also includes other pieces that wander from the straight and narrow path of orthodox economics, straying into political science and other fields. This is the most unconventional of development economists, now an honoured member of the academic establishment in spite of himself, firing on all cylinders.

As well as being an influential work in development theory and policy, Michael Lipton's *Why Poor People Stay Poor* (Temple Smith, 1976) is a model economics book. It examines the urban bias in poor-country growth – the tendency for rising incomes to drive capital and labour from the countryside, where they are relatively productive, into the towns, where they are not; this biased pattern of development leaves many people poorer than they were at the outset. Mr Lipton draws on his exceptionally broad knowledge of developing countries to build new theoretical models, then tests them with facts and figures. He writes simply and clearly.

Clear and simple books on the theory of growth in industrial economies are much harder to find. A good place to start would be the chapters on growth in Branson's *Macroeconomic Theory and Policy*. The lectures in Robert Solow's little book, *Growth Theory: An Exposition* (Oxford University Press, 1970) are a teaching *tour de force*, but even Mr Solow cannot make the subject easy. This seems to be one area where it is impossible for the mathematically unsophisticated to make much progress.

Mathematics and econometrics

Anybody who wants to delve seriously into any branch of economic theory needs to know some maths. Fortunately, in economics, a little maths goes a very long way, so the effort can be well worth while. There are plenty of maths-for-social-science cookbooks, and little to choose between most of them. They all equip the reader with the basics: differential calculus (vital in every branch of the subject), integral calculus (for financial theory and growth models), matrix algebra (for manipulating systems of many equations), mathematical optimization (the most important tool for microeconomics), and a smattering of set theory (as a preparation for mathematical statistics).

Alpha Chiang's *Fundamental Methods of Mathematical Economics* (McGraw Hill, 1967) stands out from the crowd. It is longer than most, without covering much extra ground, because the author starts from scratch and takes great pains to talk the student through each new technique. And he provides copious worked examples drawn from economic theory. Chiang's is one of the few books in this category that is suitable for teach-yourself students. Those who have done all this before, however, or learned their maths in a different field (engineering, say) could get by with a refresher; for this, Stephen Glaister's crisp *Mathematical Methods for Economists* (Basil Blackwell, 1978) will do.

Econometrics is not the same thing as mathematical economics; it is a branch of statistics devoted to testing economic hypotheses. Most professional economic forecasters know very little econometric theory; they insist on using fairly simple techniques that the few in the know can denounce in their own minority-interest journals. Those with a taste for the hard stuff must know their matrix algebra first, as well as some elementary statistical theory; then they might try John Johnston's *Econometric Methods* (McGraw Hill, 1963) – for years this has been a set text at the London School of Economics and elsewhere.

An easier book – it relegates matrix notation to appendices, and is generally much more reader-friendly – is *Econometric*

Models and Economic Forecasts, by Robert Pindyck and Daniel Rubinfeld (McGraw Hill, 1980). This book is also recommended for the insight it gives into the art of simulation – running hypothetical forecasts on the basis of assumed changes in policy. But the best book by far on the non-statistical aspects of model-building is Michael Evans's *Macroeconomic Activity* (Harper and Row, 1969). As well as describing the elements of a large-scale model that Evans himself constructed, it is one of the few modern textbooks that has anything to say about business cycles – these continue to fascinate commentators and financial markets, if not most academics.

Microeconomics

Except in chapter 14, this book has ignored microeconomics. Readers who want to shirk the maths, but would like to read more micro might try David Laidler's *Introduction to Microeconomics* (Philip Allan, 1981). The exposition rests on geometry rather than algebra; this makes the book more accessible to those who are willing to stare at complicated charts. Laidler writes clearly, although some issues are fudged in the interest of simplicity. The range of topics is standard: consumer theory; theory of the firm; demand for factors of production; perfect and imperfect competition; and general equilibrium theory.

A more advanced book, which relies on mathematical notation and elementary maths techniques throughout, is *Microeconomic Theory*, by Alan Walters and Richard Layard (McGraw Hill, 1978). It covers the same issues as Laidler's book, but in much greater depth, and with an emphasis on methods that the student can apply himself. Exercises at the end of each chapter pose refreshingly concrete problems which, the authors hope, students can use the theory to answer. For example, 'Suppose all subsidies on education beyond the age of 18 were abolished; what would be the effect on the inequality of personal incomes?'

General equilibrium theory can be very hard; Frank Hahn,

one of Britain's most brilliant theoretical economists, has written some terrifying papers on the subject. Fortunately, he has also written an elegant little essay for a collection called *The Crisis in Economic Theory*, edited by Daniel Bell and Irving Kristol (Basic Books, 1982). The book is worth buying for Hahn's piece alone – in sixteen non-technical pages it explains that the theory, though a marvellous intellectual achievement, cannot support the weight of policy conclusions that have been built on it, and that economics is moving in a direction that will overturn many of those conclusions. The volume also has some interesting articles by Allan Meltzer, Kenneth Arrow and others. (None of them justifies that alarmist title.)

The little-read classic of game theory is *The Theory of Games and Economic Behaviour*, by John von Neumann and Oskar Morgenstern (Princeton University Press, 1944). *Games and Decisions*, by Duncan Luce and Howard Raiffa (Wiley, 1957), is much more approachable, but still quite hard in places. A newer book by Martin Shubik – *Game Theory in the Social Sciences: Concepts and Solutions* (M.I.T. Press, 1982) – is more up-to-date, and often clearer than the one by Luce and Raiffa. But the best non-technical introduction to the sorts of economic problem that game theory tries to handle is Thomas Schelling's *Micromotives and Macrobehaviour* (Norton, 1980). The book looks at bargaining and other forms of economic and social conflict, and at the problems they create when society tries to aggregate the decisions of individuals. Of all academic economists, Mr Schelling is probably the leading inventor of ingenious and entertaining examples.

Ray Rees's *Public Enterprise Economics* (Weidenfeld and Nicolson, 1976) explains the problems of efficient resource allocation under a particular kind of imperfect competition – publicly-owned natural monopoly. The book has clear chapters on two tricky issues: the principle of marginal-cost pricing, and the problems of second-best policy (i.e. how to achieve economic efficiency when conditions for efficiency elsewhere in the economy are not met). Mr Rees derives all his results formally in mathematical appendices; so the text is unencumbered. This is one area where apparently abstract economic theory can have a direct bearing on economic policy.

More abstract theorizing in Amartya Sen's *Collective Choice and Social Welfare* (North-Holland, 1979). This book goes deeply into the problems of deriving economic rules for society from the preferences of its individual members. It explores the Arrow Impossibility Theorem and the Paradox of Voting in detail – both of these were mentioned in chapter 14. Such issues take this classic work outside the normal boundaries of economics, into the realms of moral and political philosophy. Sen rules this borderline terrain unchallenged. His book is hard, and employs methods of formal logic which are only sketched in the first chapter. But it follows the unusual convention of alternating non-technical, descriptive chapters with starred chapters that restate the argument in formal notation; by reading the non-starred chapters, technical weaklings can get a good grasp of the arguments.

Index

A CHOICE OF
PELICANS AND PEREGRINES

☐ **The Knight, the Lady and the Priest**
  Georges Duby   £6.95

The acclaimed study of the making of modern marriage in medieval France. 'He has traced this story – sometimes amusing, often horrifying, always startling – in a series of brilliant vignettes' – *Observer*

☐ **The Limits of Soviet Power** **Jonathan Steele**   £3.95

The Kremlin's foreign policy – Brezhnev to Chernenko, is discussed in this informed, informative 'wholly invaluable and extraordinarily timely study' – *Guardian*

☐ **Understanding Organizations** **Charles B. Handy**   £4.95

Third Edition. Designed as a practical source-book for managers, this Pelican looks at the concepts, key issues and current fashions in tackling organizational problems.

☐ **The Pelican Freud Library: Volume 12**   £5.95

Containing the major essays: *Civilization, Society and Religion, Group Psychology* and *Civilization and Its Discontents*, plus other works.

☐ **Windows on the Mind** **Erich Harth**   £4.95

Is there a physical explanation for the various phenomena that we call 'mind'? Professor Harth takes in age-old philosophers as well as the latest neuroscientific theories in his masterly study of memory, perception, free will, selfhood, sensation and other richly controversial fields.

☐ **The Pelican History of the World**
  J. M. Roberts   £5.95

'A stupendous achievement . . . This is the unrivalled World History for our day' – A. J. P. Taylor

A CHOICE OF
PELICANS AND PEREGRINES

☐ *A Question of Economics* **Peter Donaldson** £4.95

Twenty key issues – from the City and big business to trades unions –
clarified and discussed by Peter Donaldson, author of *10 × Economics* and one of our greatest popularizers of economics.

☐ *Inside the Inner City* **Paul Harrison** £4.95

A report on urban poverty and conflict by the author of *Inside the Third World*. 'A major piece of evidence' – *Sunday Times*. 'A classic: it tells us what it is really like to be poor, and why' – *Time Out*

☐ *What Philosophy Is* **Anthony O'Hear** £4.95

What are human beings? How should people act? How do our thoughts and words relate to reality? Contemporary attitudes to these age-old questions are discussed in this new study, an eloquent and brilliant introduction to philosophy today.

☐ *The Arabs* **Peter Mansfield** £4.95

New Edition. 'Should be studied by anyone who wants to know about the Arab world and how the Arabs have become what they are today' – *Sunday Times*

☐ *Religion and the Rise of Capitalism*
   R. H. Tawney £3.95

The classic study of religious thought of social and economic issues from the later middle ages to the early eighteenth century.

☐ *The Mathematical Experience*
   Philip J. Davis and Reuben Hersh £7.95

Not since *Gödel, Escher, Bach* has such an entertaining book been written on the relationship of mathematics to the arts and sciences. 'It deserves to be read by everyone ... an instant classic' – *New Scientist*

PENGUIN REFERENCE BOOKS

☐ *The Penguin Map of the World*   £2.95

Clear, colourful, crammed with information and fully up-to-date, this is a useful map to stick on your wall at home, at school or in the office.

☐ *The Penguin Map of Europe*   £2.95

Covers all land eastwards to the Urals, southwards to North Africa and up to Syria, Iraq and Iran * Scale = 1:5,500,000 * 4-colour artwork * Features main roads, railways, oil and gas pipelines, plus extra information including national flags, currencies and populations.

☐ *The Penguin Map of the British Isles*   £2.95

Including the Orkneys, the Shetlands, the Channel Islands and much of Normandy, this excellent map is ideal for planning routes and touring holidays, or as a study aid.

☐ *The Penguin Dictionary of Quotations*   £3.95

A treasure-trove of over 12,000 new gems and old favourites, from Aesop and Matthew Arnold to Xenophon and Zola.

☐ *The Penguin Dictionary of Art and Artists*   £3.95

Fifth Edition. 'A vast amount of information intelligently presented, carefully detailed, abreast of current thought and scholarship and easy to read' – *The Times Literary Supplement*

☐ *The Penguin Pocket Thesaurus*   £2.50

A pocket-sized version of Roget's classic, and an essential companion for all commuters, crossword addicts, students, journalists and the stuck-for-words.

PENGUIN REFERENCE BOOKS

☐ *The Penguin Dictionary of Troublesome Words*   £2.50

A witty, straightforward guide to the pitfalls and hotly disputed issues in standard written English, illustrated with examples and including a glossary of grammatical terms and an appendix on punctuation.

☐ *The Penguin Guide to the Law*   £8.95

This acclaimed reference book is designed for everyday use, and forms the most comprehensive handbook ever published on the law as it affects the individual.

☐ *The Penguin Dictionary of Religions*   £4.95

The rites, beliefs, gods and holy books of all the major religions throughout the world are covered in this book, which is illustrated with charts, maps and line drawings.

☐ *The Penguin Medical Encyclopedia*   £4.95

Covers the body and mind in sickness and in health, including drugs, surgery, history, institutions, medical vocabulary and many other aspects. Second Edition. 'Highly commendable' – *Journal of the Institute of Health Education*

☐ *The Penguin Dictionary of Physical Geography*   £4.95

This book discusses all the main terms used, in over 5,000 entries illustrated with diagrams and meticulously cross-referenced.

☐ *Roget's Thesaurus*   £3.50

Specially adapted for Penguins, Sue Lloyd's acclaimed new version of Roget's original will help you find the right words for your purposes. 'As normal a part of an intelligent household's library as the Bible, Shakespeare or a dictionary' – *Daily Telegraph*

A CHOICE OF PENGUINS

☐ **The Complete Penguin Stereo Record and Cassette Guide**
  Greenfield, Layton and March   £7.95

A new edition, now including information on compact discs. 'One of the few indispensables on the record collector's bookshelf' – *Gramophone*

☐ **Selected Letters of Malcolm Lowry**
  Edited by Harvey Breit and Margerie Bonner Lowry £5.95

'Lowry emerges from these letters not only as an extremely interesting man, but also a lovable one' – Philip Toynbee

☐ **The First Day on the Somme**
  Martin Middlebrook   £3.95

1 July 1916 was the blackest day of slaughter in the history of the British Army. 'The soldiers receive the best service a historian can provide: their story told in their own words' – *Guardian*

☐ **A Better Class of Person** **John Osborne**   £2.50

The playwright's autobiography, 1929–56. 'Splendidly enjoyable' – John Mortimer. 'One of the best, richest and most bitterly truthful autobiographies that I have ever read' – Melvyn Bragg

☐ **The Winning Streak** **Goldsmith and Clutterbuck** £2.95

Marks & Spencer, Saatchi & Saatchi, United Biscuits, GEC ... The UK's top companies reveal their formulas for success, in an important and stimulating book that no British manager can afford to ignore.

☐ **The First World War** **A. J. P. Taylor**   £4.95

'He manages in some 200 illustrated pages to say almost everything that is important ... A special text ... a remarkable collection of photographs' – *Observer*

A CHOICE OF PENGUINS

PENGUIN TRAVEL BOOKS

☐ *Arabian Sands* **Wilfred Thesiger** £3.95

'In the tradition of Burton, Doughty, Lawrence, Philby and Thomas, it is, very likely, the book about Arabia to end all books about Arabia' – *Daily Telegraph*

☐ *The Flight of Ikaros* **Kevin Andrews** £3.50

'He also is in love with the country . . . but he sees the other side of that dazzling medal or moon . . . If you want some truth about Greece, here it is' – Louis MacNeice in the *Observer*

☐ *D. H. Lawrence and Italy* £4.95

In *Twilight in Italy, Sea and Sardinia* and *Etruscan Places,* Lawrence recorded his impressions while living, writing and travelling in 'one of the most beautiful countries in the world'.

☐ *Maiden Voyage* **Denton Welch** £3.95

Opening during his last term at public school, from which the author absconded, *Maiden Voyage* turns into a brilliantly idiosyncratic account of China in the 1930s.

☐ *The Grand Irish Tour* **Peter Somerville-Large** £4.95

The account of a year's journey round Ireland. 'Marvellous . . . describes to me afresh a landscape I thought I knew' – Edna O'Brien in the *Observer*

☐ *Slow Boats to China* **Gavin Young** £3.95

On an ancient steamer, a cargo dhow, a Filipino kumpit and twenty more agreeably cranky boats, Gavin Young sailed from Piraeus to Canton in seven crowded and colourful months. 'A pleasure to read' – Paul Theroux

PENGUIN TRAVEL BOOKS

☐ *The Kingdom by the Sea* **Paul Theroux**   £2.50

1982, the year of the Falklands War and the Royal Baby, was the ideal
time, Theroux found, to travel round the coast of Britain and surprise
the British into talking about themselves. 'He describes it all brilliantly and honestly' – Anthony Burgess

☐ *One's Company* **Peter Fleming**   £3.50

His journey to China as special correspondent to *The Times* in 1933.
'One reads him for literary delight . . . But, he is also an observer of
penetrating intellect' – Vita Sackville West

☐ *The Traveller's Tree* **Patrick Leigh Fermor**   £3.95

'A picture of the Indies more penetrating and original than any that
has been presented before' – *Observer*

☐ *The Path to Rome* **Hilaire Belloc**   £3.95

'The only book I ever wrote for love,' is how Belloc described the
wonderful blend of anecdote, humour and reflection that makes up
the story of his pilgrimage to Rome.

☐ *The Light Garden of the Angel King* **Peter Levi**   £2.95

Afghanistan has been a wild rocky highway for nomads and mer-
chants, Alexander the Great, Buddhist monks, great Moghul con-
querors and the armies of the Raj. Here, quite brilliantly, Levi writes
about their journeys and his own.

☐ *Among the Russians* **Colin Thubron**   £3.95

'The Thubron approach to travelling has an integrity that belongs to
another age' – Dervla Murphy in the *Irish Times*. 'A magnificent
achievement' – Nikolai Tolstoy

PENGUINS ON HEALTH, SPORT AND KEEPING FIT

☐ *Medicines* **Peter Parish**   £4.95

Fifth Edition. The usages, dosages and adverse effects of all medicines obtainable on prescription or over the counter are covered in this reference guide, designed for the ordinary reader and everyone in health care.

☐ *Baby & Child* **Penelope Leach**   £7.95

A fully illustrated, expert and comprehensive handbook on the first five years of life. 'It stands head and shoulders above anything else available at the moment' – Mary Kenny in the *Spectator*

☐ *Vogue Natural Health and Beauty*
Bronwen Meredith   £7.50

Health foods, yoga, spas, recipes, natural remedies and beauty preparations are all included in this superb, fully illustrated guide and companion to the bestselling *Vogue Body and Beauty Book.*

☐ *Pregnancy and Diet* **Rachel Holme**   £1.95

With suggested foods, a sample diet-plan of menus and advice on nutrition, this guide shows you how to avoid excessive calories but still eat well and healthily during pregnancy.

☐ *The Penguin Bicycle Handbook* **Rob van der Plas**   £4.95

Choosing a bicycle, maintenance, accessories, basic tools, safety, keeping fit – all these subjects and more are covered in this popular, fully illustrated guide to the total bicycle lifestyle.

☐ *Physical Fitness*   £1.25

Containing the 5BX 11-minute-a-day plan for men and the XBX 12-minute-a-day plan for women, this book illustrates the famous programmes originally developed by the Royal Canadian Air Force and now used successfully all over the world.